A toast to sober spirits & joyous juices

Y0-DBS-029

A toast to sober spirits

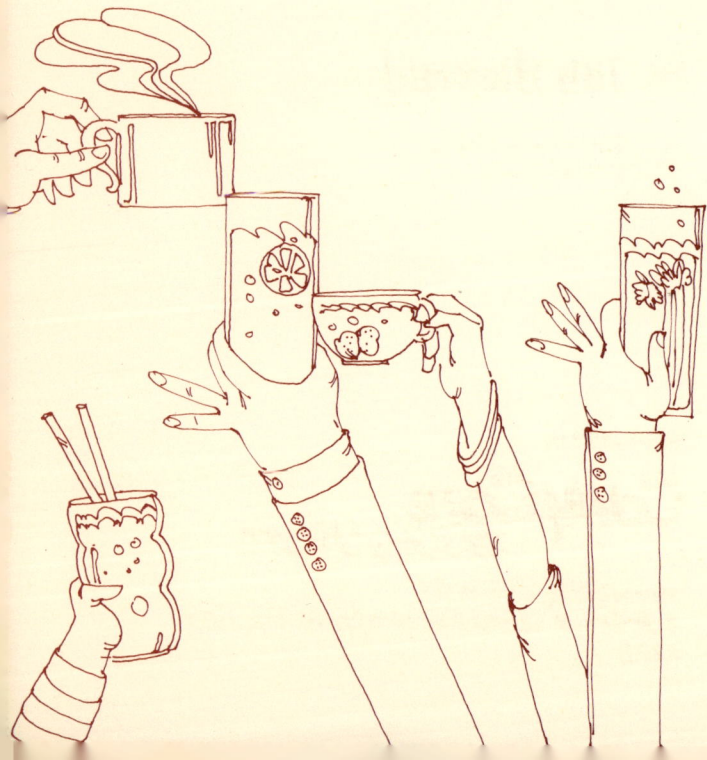

& joyous juices

by Jan Blexrud

Illustrated by Robert Kilbride
Cover by Goose Graphics

Published by

CompCare publications

Minneapolis, Minnesota
A division of Comprehensive Care Corporation
1976

© 1976 by Janet C. Blexrud

All rights reserved.
Published in the United States
by CompCare Publications.

Library of Congress Catalog Card
No. 76-55449

Reproduction in whole or part, in
any form, including storage in
memory device or system, is
forbidden without written
permission . . . except that portions
may be used in broadcast or printed
commentary or review when
attributed fully to author and
publication by names.

To all my friends who remained enthusiastic, drank the unending flow of experimental drinks and waited patiently for this compilation to roll off the press. And to Tom, Sarah and Adam who relinquished the dining room to this project and ate their meals for seven months crowded around the kitchen table.

Contents

Foreword

This book is the product of two of my frustrations which surfaced simultaneously last winter. One was an awareness that the long Minnesota winter **still** seemed interminable, regardless of how many hours I skated or skied. The other was total boredom with plain old coffee and plain old tea and plain old soft drinks coupled with an inability to locate suitable recipes for refreshing and appetizing non-alcoholic drinks to replace the old boring standards. My collection of sixty cookbooks was woefully sparse in this category, and a search of bookstores turned up **not one single** cookbook filled with non-alcoholic beverage recipes.

When I casually suggested the need for such a book to a number of my friends and acquaintances, the response was overwhelming. It certainly appeared that many others felt the same frustration I did. That settled it — if the book was needed, then it should be created.

As March blizzards blew, I stashed my skis and began the months of research, aided by a steady stream of recipe contributions from friends throughout the country. Then came hours of pouring, measuring, mixing, stirring, experimenting and sampling before the entire collection was finally assembled.

Throughout this whole process, I have discovered new freedoms — the freedom to mix drinks appropriate for every occasion and for every age group without using alcoholic ingredients and the freedom to experiment successfully with new kinds of foods.

And so — here's to freedom, to choice and to you! Read, experiment and enjoy.

How to use this book

There are two ways you can use this book: First, in a purely utilitarian sense by selecting a recipe, trying it out and putting the book away until next time. Or second, in a more pleasurable sense by sitting down with it, paging through and taking the time to appreciate all that is offered. As its author, I encourage you to take the latter course; I think you'll be glad you did for I have included information from personal experience and from the suggestions of many others that I am certain will be as useful to you as it's been to me and to them.

Section one Getting It All Together, acquaints you with definitions used in this book, equipment recommended and new ways to make drinks more appealing, all designed to aid you as you try the recipes.

Section two The Recipes, instructs you in expert drink mixing whether you're preparing a carbonated beverage for one or brewing a hot concoction for a crowd. The headings in this section divide the 300 plus recipes into convenient categories for easy reference. Also included are a few "go-with" recipes and extra information "tidbits" for your additional pleasure.

Section three The Appendices, helps you find what you're looking for. Especially helpful is the ingredient reference guide which directs you to the proper recipe when you don't know what to do with juices or other ingredients. By following the ingredient columns you will find the name and page of recipes using them. Measurement charts for calories, metrics, and equivalents are also in this section.

Getting it all together

Definitions of mixing terminology, equipment for mixing drinks, heating drinks, serving drinks. Treatment of glassware. Garnishes. Ices. And other hints.

Definitions
of drink mixing terms
as used in this book.

Ade / A tall, frosty drink made of fruit juice and plain or soda water, garnished with fresh fruit slices.

Beat / To place in an electric mixer and mix until smoothly combined.

Blend / To place in an electric blender and mix at a designated speed.

Carbonated water / Effervescent drink which is highly charged with carbonic gas.

Cobbler / A tall drink with fresh fruit and crushed ice, sometimes garnished with fresh mint.

Collins / A tall drink of sugar and lemon or lime juice with a carbonated beverage poured over ice.

Combine / To mix thoroughly.

Cooler / A tall drink with fruit flavoring, fruit rind, cracked ice and a carbonated beverage.

Daisy / A drink with grenadine and lemon or lime juice shaken with cracked ice and served with a fruit garnish.

Dash / A short quick shake of a given ingredient.

Demitasse / A small, 1 or 2 ounce cup which is used for serving hot, strongly flavored drinks.

Dollop / A heaping spoonful of creamy mixture which is plopped on top of a drink.

Egg nog / See Nog.

Fizz / A drink made of citrus juice and syrup or sugar, shaken with ice, poured and filled with a carbonated beverage.

Fizzle / Fruit juice and a carbonated beverage.

Frappé / Fruit juices that are frozen to a slushy consistency or made with a blender and crushed ice.

Garnish / To decorate.

Gently add / To pour slowly to prevent the fizz or carbonation from escaping.

Grenadine / A syrup of pomegranates or red currants, used for its flavor and color.

Julep / A drink using fresh mint (muddled, crushed or whole) and served with crushed ice and a frosted glass.

Muddler / A stick used to crush or mix fruit slices, mint, sugar, etc. in drinks.

Mull / To heat just to the boiling point.

Nog / A drink made with whole eggs.

Orgeat / An almond flavored syrup which can be purchased in a bottle shop.

Punch / A drink made with fruit juices.

Rickey / A drink made with lime, cracked ice and carbonated beverage with a twist of lemon.

Shake / To place in a tightly covered container (a recycled peanut butter jar will do nicely!) and shake vigorously.

Smash / A drink with sprigs of mint, carbonated beverage and garnished with fruit.

Soda water / Same as carbonated water.

Sour / A drink with lemon juice, sugar and ice and garnished with a lemon slice and cherry.

Steep / To pour a hot liquid over leaves, cover and allow to sit, thus producing a flavorful and colorful brew.

Sugar syrup / A liquid made of 2 parts sugar and 1 part water which is boiled 5 minutes, cooled, and covered. Keeps indefinitely in refrigerator.

Swizzle / A cool drink with bitters, lemon or lime juice and sugar. Crushed ice is added to make it very cold.

Twist / A thin slice of citrus fruit (lemon, orange or lime).

Zest / The outside rind of citrus fruit which can be scraped off with a grater or peeled with a lemon stripper.

Equipment for mixing drinks

The following list is not meant to be a "must have" list. If your kitchen is used for daily cooking you will have most of these items in your cupboards. Blenders and ice crushers are useful but ingenuity can create functional substitutes. Small hand gadgets such as the lemon stripper or lime squeezer are not necessities but put them on your list for the next time you find yourself in a gourmet shop with the irresistible urge to buy "something."

can /bottle opener

bottle stoppers / for capping carbonated beverages

measuring spoons

measuring cups / a 4 cup glass measurement is especially useful for quantity drinks

cutting board and sharp knife / for preparing garnishes

shaker / a jar with a tight fitting cover will do (peanut butter jar works very well)

beater / electric or hand rotary

orange juice squeezer

lime squeezer

grater / small, single-sided for easy cleaning

lemon stripper / small, hand gadget for peeling the colored part from citrus fruits

strainer/pitcher

large container / for mixing quantity drinks (a commercial size mayonnaise jar can be used)

blender / electric device used for making smooth mixtures *Alternative* / Use a food mill to break up solids and then beat with rotary beater.

ice crusher / electric device used for crushing ice. *Alternative* / place ice in canvas bag or heavy towel and crush with mallet or hammer.

Equipment for heating drinks

Hot drinks can be heated in stove-top pans but don't overlook the possibility of having your automatic percolators do double duty. Use them to heat fruit and vegetable drinks by putting spices and other seasonings in the percolator basket. Perk them as you would coffee. No need to strain, simply remove the basket before pouring.

sauce pans
teapot / earthen pot for steeping
automatic percolator / 9-12 cup size
automatic percolator / 22-30 cup size

Equipment for serving drinks

It is not necessary to purchase special glassware for serving drinks. Take an inventory of what you have and go from there. Be creative; avoid limiting yourself to the conventional drinkware. One imaginative hostess serves drinks in fruit jars. Sea food icers make pleasing containers for slushy or fruity drinks. Or, let the occasion suggest the drinkware; for example, use large size baby food jars for a celebration involving parents-to-be. Do recalculate the number of servings a recipe will make according to the size of the drinkware you choose.

demitasse / 1-2 oz.
punch cup / 4 oz.
juice glass / 4-6 oz.
cup / 8 oz. with handles for hot drinks
glass / 8 oz.
tall glass / 10 oz.
very tall glass / taller than a 10 oz.
straws / Keep a good supply of long ones which can be cut shorter depending on the size of the glass.
long-handled spoons / for fruit and slush drinks
muddler / a stick used to crush mint and stir fruited drinks
punch bowl / for serving quantity drinks — If you use one infrequently, rent or borrow one or use a salad bowl, colorful mixing bowl, or even a fish bowl sans its residents. (All punch type recipes in this book can be converted easily to individual drinks if you desire.)
tray / smooth surfaced for serving drinks

Treatment of glassware

A few quick hints about glassware that will enhance the looks and palatability of your drinks.

To prechill glassware, try one of the following: for a cold glass, place in refrigerator half an hour before serving; for a heavy frost, place in freezer; for an extra heavy frost, rinse in tepid water and place in freezer for a few hours.

To decorate the rim of a glass, try one of the following: dip in egg white, then salt, shake off excess and dry; dampen rim with lemon or lime, dip in sugar, tap off excess and dry; dip rim in water, then in powdered sugar, tap off excess and dry.

For a strong, well-insulated container, use doubled-up plastic glasses.

Garnishes

Garnishes are not necessities but they do enhance the looks of a drink. They also soak up flavor and are delectable treats at the end of an already enjoyable drink. Fix garnishes ahead of time for less fuss during preparation time. When guests are mixing their own, provide an assortment of garnishes. Don't limit yourself to what the recipe suggests. If your favorite fruit is in season and it seems compatible with the drink, use it! You may come up with some tasty surprises! When using apple or banana for garnish, dip them in citrus juice to prevent discoloration. Slice fruit or vegetable garnishes about one fourth inch thick. If many fruits are available make mini-kebobs by threading several on a sturdy pick.

Garnishes for fruited drinks

apple slices / with peel on
banana / dip in citrus juice to prevent darkening
cherries / with stems intact
citrus slices / embed cloves in rind
cucumber spear / sliced length-wise
berries / fresh or frozen
grapes
melon balls
pineapple chunks
orange / sliced or rind peeled in one long strip with lemon stripper
lemon / see orange
lime / see orange
mint / leaves or sprig of leaves

cinnamon stick / for flavor and as a stir stick

candy stick / for flavor and as a stir stick

red hot candies / add to hot drinks for added color and flavor

sherbet / freeze balls of sherbet on a cookie sheet and add to drink just before serving

Garnishes for vegetable drinks

carrot sticks

celery / with leafy tops

cauliflower / small florets or thin slices

croutons / fried or toasted cubes of bread

green pepper / thin strips or small chopped pieces

green olives / stuffed with pimento

ripe olives / pitted and sliced

onion / fresh, green with stems on

sour cream / dollop

yogurt / dollop

cherry tomato

parsley / fresh sprigs

other herbs / fresh sprigs

Garnishes for coffee — see page 69

Ices

Ice, either cubed, crushed or cracked, is the basis of most cold drinks. When mixing a drink be sure the ingredients are cold, as ice is intended to keep your drink cool, not to cool the drink. Ice used for cooling produces an unsatisfactory, watery, lukewarm drink with little guest appeal! Do plan ahead and keep a good supply of ice in stock as few things are more frustrating than running out of ice before running out of guests. Colorful and tasty ice cubes can be prepared using these hints.

For clear cubes, boil water before freezing.

Use cubes as a garnish by placing curls of lemon, orange or lime peel, clove-studded orange slices, cherries with stems, fruit chunks, cherry tomatoes, mint leaves, or anything else you think would be attractive in the trays before freezing.

Make cubes of fruit juices to prevent dilution of drinks. Pineapple juice is especially good. This is a good way to use leftover juices.

Add food coloring or grenadine for colorful cubes.

To remove ice from trays let them sit at room temperature for a few minutes. (Running warm water over them will cause them to stick together.)

For an interesting punch bowl garland: Fill a ring mold with one inch of water and freeze, add fruits, barely cover with water and freeze again. Finally, fill to the top with water and freeze. To remove, set mold in hot water for a few seconds.

Punch bowl rings can also be made from the punch itself. Use the above procedure if you wish to add fruits.

Do discard old ice as it may have absorbed unpleasant odors.

Dry ice is exotic but handle with care! Store in a metal container and handle with tongs, adding only a cupful at a time. Too much can crack a glass bowl or freeze up a drink.

Lemon juice helps clear up a "muddy" drink.

Food coloring or grenadine provides a color boost.

Premixing enhances the mellowness of a drink. Mix all but the carbonated ingredients and refrigerate for a few hours in a covered glass container.

When serving drinks before a meal, do not serve very sweet drinks or those heavy with cream or egg.

Heavily garnished and slushy-type drinks look good in tall, clear glassware.

Quantities and Such

1 orange	6-8 tbsp. juice, 2-3 tbsp. rind
1 lemon	2-3 tbsp. juice, 2 tsp. rind
1 lime	1½-2 tbsp. juice, 1½ tsp. rind
1 tray ice	1 quart crushed ice
1 cup cream	2 cups whipped cream
1 pineapple	2 cups pineapple juice (approx.)
1 medium banana	⅓-½ cup mashed banana
1 clove garlic	1/8 tsp. garlic powder
1 tbsp. fresh horseradish	2 tbsp. bottled horseradish
¼ gr. saccharin	1 tsp. sugar

Metric Conversion Chart

1 teaspoon	5 milliliters
1 tablespoon	15 milliliters
1 cup	¼ liter, approx.
1 pint	.4732 liters
1 quart	.9463 liters
1 gallon	3.785 liters

Liquid Measure Volume Equivalents

A few grains	Less than 1/8 teaspoon
60 drops	1 teaspoon
1 teaspoon	⅓ tablespoon
1 tablespoon	3 teaspoons
2 tablespoons	1 fluid ounce
4 tablespoons	¼ cup
5⅓ tablespoons	⅓ cup
8 tablespoons	½ cup
16 tablespoons	1 cup or 8 ounces
8 tablespoons	4 ounces
¼ cup	4 tablespoons
3/8 cup	¼ cup plus 2 tablespoons
5/8 cup	½ cup plus 2 tablespoons
7/8 cup	¾ cup plus 2 tablespoons
1 cup	½ pint or 8 fluid ounces
2 cups	1 pint
1 pint	16 fluid ounces
1 quart	2 pints
1 gallon	4 quarts

Serve nibblers with your drinks

Easy, tasty food accompaniments.

Sea Delight

1   (6½ oz.) can tuna
1   (6½ oz.) can crabmeat
1   (8 oz.) can clams
1   (4½ oz.) can shrimp
2½ cup thinly sliced celery
¼   cup grated onion
1   (2 oz.) jar pimento
½   cup mayonnaise
½   cup sour cream
1½ tbsp. lemon juice
salt to taste
pepper to taste
3   hard cooked eggs, quartered
dill

Drain and rinse seafoods. Combine seafoods, celery, onion and pimento in bowl. In separate container mix mayonnaise, sour cream and lemon juice. Pour over seafoods and gently mix. Add salt and pepper. Refrigerate for an hour before serving. Garnish with eggs and sprinkle with dill. Serves 6 or 8.

Crabmeat Dip

8   oz. cream cheese
3   tbsp. horseradish
1   (7½ oz.) can crabmeat
1   tbsp. catsup

Drain crabmeat. Combine with other ingredients and chill. Serve with garlic bread chips.

Shrimp Pot

1½ lb. cooked shrimp
⅓   cup chopped onion
2   tbsp. finely chopped parsley
⅔   cup salad oil
⅓   cup vinegar
1/8 tsp. garlic powder
1½ tsp. salt
1/8 tsp. pepper

Combine shrimp, onion and parsley in large bowl. In separate container mix other ingredients as dressing. Gently mix to combine. Let sit in refrigerator for at least 24 hours before serving. This will keep for several days and is even more delicious as the flavors blend — but be sure to keep it refrigerated at all times. Serve with crackers.

Party Crunch

1½ cups melted butter
¼   cup Worcestershire sauce
2   tsp. garlic salt
2   tsp. onion salt
1/8 tsp. garlic powder
1   lb. nuts
6   cups toasted oat cereal
6   cups crisp rice cereal
12 cups shredded wheat squares
6   cups pretzel sticks

Melt butter and combine with Worcestershire sauce and other seasonings. Set aside. Combine nuts with other ingredients and spread on baking sheet. Pour butter sauce over and bake in 250° oven for 2 hours. Stir every 20-30 minutes. Cool and drain on heavy brown paper.

Super Chips

Preheat oven to 350°. Dust potato chips with a favorite herb, curry powder or chili powder. Sprinkle with garlic salt or onion salt. Spread on cookie sheet and heat for 5 minutes. Serve warm.

Mini Pizza

Mozzarella cheese
tomato sauce
oregano
Parmesan cheese
crackers

Preheat oven to 400°. Top crackers with thin slices of Mozzarella cheese. Spread with tomato sauce, sprinkle with oregano and Parmesan. Bake for 10 minutes. Serve immediately.

Pretzel Dip

1 lb. pasteurized processed
**   American cheese spread**
¼ cup hot milk
poppy seeds
pretzel sticks

Melt cheese and add milk. Dip pretzel sticks into cheese mixture, then in poppy seeds. Serve. This mixture can be put in a small chafing dish and guests can dip their own pretzel sticks.

Tasty Bread Sticks

1 (8 oz.) pkg. refrigerator biscuits
¼ cup butter or margarine
garlic powder
Parmesan cheese

Preheat oven to 400°. Melt butter in baking pan. Separate biscuits and roll into long thin shapes. Roll in butter, setting in place in baking pan. Sprinkle with garlic powder and Parmesan cheese. Bake for 10 min.

Sandwich Toasts

½ green pepper
3 tbsp. chopped onion
8 oz. sharp cheddar cheese
1 can Spam
1 (4 oz.) can tomato paste

Chop or grind pepper, onion, cheese and Spam. Combine with tomato paste. Toast one side of bread. Spread mixture on other side and broil until brown. (Watch carefully to prevent burning!)

Cucumber Celery Chop

½ cup finely chopped cucumber
½ cup finely chopped celery
salt to taste
onion salt to taste

Combine ingredients, refrigerate for an hour before serving. Serve with crackers or toasted circles of bread.

Cauliflower Tidbits

1 head cauliflower
salt
French dressing
parsley

Remove outer leaves and any bruised or brown spots from head of cauliflower. Break flowerets into bite-sized pieces. Bring 1 inch salted water to boil and add cauliflower. Reduce heat, cover and simmer for 8 minutes, or until tender but slightly crisp. Do not overcook! Drain and place in glass bowl. Drizzle with dressing, toss to coat and marinate covered in refrigerator for several hours. Roll in parsley before serving.

Celery Sticks

celery sticks
1 (8 oz.) pkg. cream cheese
1 pkg. onion soup mix
¼ tsp. garlic salt

Combine cheese, dry soup mix and salt. Fill celery sticks. Serve.

Crunch Cheese Sticks

bread (day old)
melted butter
Parmesan cheese

Cut bread into one by three inch strips. Dip bread in butter and then in Parmesan cheese. Broil, turning as they brown. Serve warm.

Creamy Fruit Dip

1¾ cup marshmallow cream
8 oz. cream cheese
1/8 tsp. ground ginger

Combine ingredients, chill and serve. Use as a dip for fruits of your choice (strawberries, melon balls, apple slices, etc.)

Shrimp Dip

8 oz. cream cheese
¼ cup cream (half and half)
2 tsp. lemon juice
¼ tsp. onion juice
dash Worcestershire sauce
¾ cup canned shrimp

Drain and chop shrimp. Add other ingredients, chill and serve. Use with chips or spread on crackers.

Braunschweiger Spread

2 cups sour cream
10 oz. braunschweiger sausage
1 pkg. dry onion soup mix
½ tsp. Worcestershire sauce
dash of hot pepper sauce

Combine ingredients, chill and serve. Use as a dip for chips or vegetables. Can also be used as a cracker spread.

Dilly Dip

1 pkg. dry onion soup mix
2 cups sour cream
1 chopped tomato
1 diced green pepper
¼ tsp. dill

Combine ingredients, chill and serve. Use with crackers or chips.

Spicy Cheese Log

1 (3 oz.) pkg. cream cheese
8 oz. sharp processed American cheese
1 tbsp. lemon juice
¼ tsp. garlic powder
dash of cayenne
⅓ cup chopped pecans (or other nuts)
½ tsp. chili powder
¼ tsp. paprika

Let cheeses soften, then add lemon juice, garlic powder and cayenne. Beat until light and stir in nuts. Roll into log shape and sprinkle with chili powder and paprika. Chill. Before serving allow to sit at room temperature for a few minutes. Slice and serve with crackers.

Checker Board Dip

2 cups sour cream
2 cups chopped ripe olives
2 diced pimentos
2 tbsp. minced onion
½ tsp. lemon juice
garlic powder to taste
dash of cayenne

Combine ingredients, chill and
serve.

India Dip

¼ cup mayonnaise
¼ cup sour cream
1 tbsp. prepared mustard
1 tbsp. sugar
¼ tsp. salt
¼ tsp. pepper
curry powder to taste

Combine ingredients, chill and
serve. Use as dip for vegetables of
your choice (zucchini, carrots,
white radishes, cauliflower, etc.)

Spinach Spread

fresh spinach
sour cream

Rinse and dry fresh spinach. Shred
into small pieces. Moisten with
small amount of sour cream. Set
next to a bowl of crackers and let
guests spread their own.

Blue Cheese Ball

1 (5 oz.) jar sharp processed
  cheese
8 oz. cream cheese
1½ oz. Roquefort or blue cheese
1 tsp. Worcestershire sauce
1/8 tsp. garlic powder
¼ cup chopped ripe olive
½ cup chopped nuts

Combine until smooth the cheeses,
Worcestershire sauce and garlic
powder. Add olives and mix. Shape
into ball and roll in nuts. Cover
and refrigerate. Serve with wheat
crackers or others of your choice.
Keeps for several weeks if covered
and refrigerated.

Rumaki

1 (6½ oz.) can water chestnuts
½ lb. bacon
½ cup soy sauce
½ cup brown sugar

Combine sugar and soy sauce.
Pour mixture over chestnuts and
marinate for an hour. Cut bacon in
strips long enough to wrap around
chestnuts. Drain chestnuts, wrap
in bacon and secure with tooth-
pick. Bake in 350° oven for 20
minutes.

Crab Relish

1 (7½ oz.) can crab meat
2 tbsp. parsley
1½ tbsp. chopped onion
1 tbsp. lemon juice
¾ tsp. curry powder

Combine all ingredients, chill and
serve with crackers.

Mix a fizzler . . .

Drinks prepared with carbonated beverages.

Fizzling drinks are easy to mix one at a time. The fizzle comes from the carbonated beverages such as ginger ale, tonic water or bitter lemon. A brief description of each of these bottled beverages is followed by a group of recipes using them. Be sure the liquids are well chilled before mixing. When adding the carbonated beverage, pour gently to preserve the fizz. It is fun to experiment with these drinks. Mix and taste. If it doesn't tickle your palate, add a little more of one or another ingredient until the combination pleases you. Or, take your favorite OTC (over the counter) pop and squeeze a twist of fresh lemon or grapefruit into it. Kids will have fun with these. Start them off on orange juice and ginger ale — a sparkling treat for anyone.

Ginger ale gets its name and its tanginess from a ginger flavored syrup which is combined with carbonated water.

Pineapple Orange Fizzle

2   **tbsp. orange juice**
2   **tbsp. pineapple juice**
ginger ale
ice cubes

Place 3-4 ice cubes in tall glass and add orange and pineapple juices. Fill with ginger ale.

Rosied Ale Twist

½   **cup ginger ale**
½   **tsp. grenadine**
slice of orange
twist of lemon
ice cubes

Place 3-4 ice cubes in glass. Add ginger ale and grenadine. Stir gently. Garnish with lemon peel and orange twist.

Cherry Pink

ginger ale
dash of grenadine
crushed ice
maraschino cherry

Fill 6 oz. glass half full of crushed ice. Pour grenadine over ice and fill with ginger ale. Garnish with cherry.

Bittersting

ginger ale
1   **tsp bitters**
ice cubes

Place 3-4 ice cubes in tall glass. Add bitters and fill with ginger ale.

Summer Swizzle

ginger ale
½   **tsp. sugar**
2   **dashes bitters**
2   **tbsp. lemon juice**
crushed ice

Fill tall glass with crushed ice. Add lemon juice, sugar and bitters. Stir to mix. Gently add ginger ale.

Ginger Ale Smash

ginger ale
1   **tbsp. root beer syrup**
slice of lemon
sprig of mint
crushed ice

Fill tall glass one third full of crushed ice. Add ginger ale, syrup and lemon. Stir gently. Garnish with mint.

Derby Zest

1   **lemon rind**
slices of lemon
ginger ale
ice cubes

Peel rind of lemon in unbroken spiral. Place rind in very tall glass with one end hooked over the rim. Add 3-4 ice cubes and a few slices of lemon. Fill with ginger ale.

Grape Zest

1 lemon
⅓ cup grape juice
ginger ale
sugar to taste
½ cup crushed ice

Peel rind as for above Derby Zest and place in glass with end hooked over rim. Squeeze juice from peeled lemon. Shake lemon juice, grape juice and sugar with crushed ice. Pour into glass and fill with ginger ale. Stir gently.

Spiced Ale

ginger ale
3 slices orange
1 tsp. lemon juice
crushed ice
powdered ginger

Gently pour ½ cup ginger ale and lemon juice over orange slices and set in cool place for several hours. Fill tall glass one third full of crushed ice and add orange mixture. Fill with ginger ale. Sprinkle with powdered ginger.

Orange Cooler

¼ cup orange juice
⅓ cup cider
½ cup crushed ice
ginger ale

Shake orange juice, cider and ice. Pour into tall glass and fill with ginger ale. Garnish with orange rind.

Mint Marvel

2 sprigs of mint
1 tsp. sugar
½ tsp. grated lemon peel
ginger ale
ice cubes

Place mint, sugar and lemon peel in tall glass. Add a little ginger ale and muddle. Add 3-4 ice cubes and fill with ginger ale.

Ginger Ale Collins

2 tbsp. sugar syrup (see pg. 5)
juice of 1 lemon
ginger ale
ice cubes

Mix sugar syrup and lemon juice in bottom of tall glass. Add 3-4 ice cubes and fill with ginger ale. Serve with a muddler.

Crackling Lemon

juice of 1 lemon
1 tsp. sugar
slice of lemon
ginger ale
½ cup crushed ice

Shake lemon juice, sugar and crushed ice together in shaker. Pour into tall glass and fill with ginger ale. Garnish with twist of lemon.

Lime Rickey

juice of 1 lime
¼ tsp. sugar
½ cup crushed ice
ginger ale
twist of lemon

Shake lime juice, sugar and cracked ice in shaker. Pour into tall glass and gently fill with ginger ale. Garnish with twist of lemon.

Grape Fizzle

2 tbsp. lemon juice
½ cup grape juice
ginger ale
ice cubes

Place 3-4 ice cubes in tall glass. Add juices and stir. Gently fill with ginger ale.

Cranberry Orange Fizzle

2   tbsp. orange juice
2   tbsp. cranberry juice
ginger ale
ice cubes

Place 3-4 ice cubes in tall glass and add orange and cranberry juices. Fill with ginger ale.

Bitter Breeze

ginger ale
½ cup root beer
dash of bitters
crushed ice

Fill tall glass half full of crushed ice. Add other ingredients and stir gently.

Summer Tan

1½ tsp. root beer syrup
slice of lemon
ginger ale
crushed ice
fresh mint

Fill tall glass one third full of crushed ice. Add syrup and lemon. Fill glass with ginger ale and stir gently. Garnish with mint if desired.

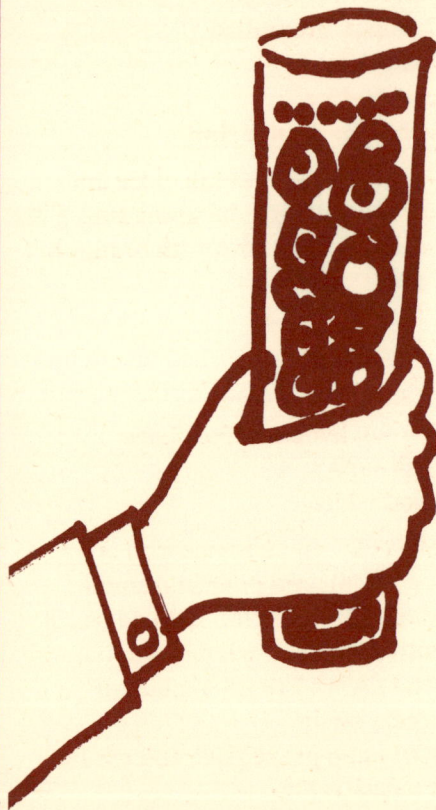

Club soda (carbonated water) is effervescent mineral water and adds zest and sparkle to mixed drinks. Drinks with club soda are appropriately called fizzes or puffs.

Club Fizzle

1   sugar cube
3   dashes of bitters
1   lemon peel
club soda
ice cubes

Peel lemon in spiral. Place sugar, bitters, lemon peel and 3-4 ice cubes in tall glass. Fill with club soda and stir gently.

Grenadine Cooler

1   tbsp. grenadine
dash of bitters
twist of lemon
club soda
crushed ice

Fill tall glass one third full of ice.
Pour grenadine over ice and add
bitters. Stir. Fill with club soda
and garnish with lemon peel.

Summer Solstice

1   tbsp. grenadine
dash of bitters
twist of lemon
club soda
crushed ice

Fill glass one third full of ice. Add
grenadine, bitters and lemon. Add
club soda and gently stir.

Creamy Lemon

⅓   cup lemon concentrate
¾   cup club soda
2   scoops vanilla ice cream

Blend until smooth. Serve immediately. Garnish with whipped cream
if desired.

Summer Pink Cooler

juice of 1 lemon
juice of ½ orange
2   tbsp. grenadine
club soda
crushed ice
lemon or orange rind

Fill tall glass half full of ice and
add fruit juices and grenadine. Fill
with soda. Garnish with orange or
lemon rind.

Almond Fizz

2   tsp. orgeat syrup
1½ tsp. lemon or lime juice
club soda
crushed ice

Shake syrup and juice with crushed
ice. Strain and pour into small
glass. Fill with club soda. Garnish
with lemon slices if desired.
ALTERNATIVES in place of
orgeat syrup:
use ¼ cup grape juice and rename
it a Grape Fizz
use 2 tsp. grenadine and call it a
Cherry Fizz.

Rosy Puff

3   tbsp. lemon juice
1½ tbsp. grenadine
club soda
ice cubes
maraschino cherry

Place 3-4 ice cubes in tall glass and
add lemon juice and grenadine.
Fill with soda and stir gently. Garnish with cherry if desired.

Lemon Fizz

⅓   cup lemon juice
1   tsp. sugar
1   cup club soda
ice cubes

Combine lemon juice and sugar in
tall glass and stir until sugar is
dissolved. Add 3-4 ice cubes and
fill with club soda.
ALTERNATIVES:
use 2 tbsp. raspberry or cherry
    syrup in place of sugar
use half grape juice and half soda
use apple juice in place of club
    soda
use lime juice in place of lemon
juice and rename Lime Fizz.

Tonic or quinine water has a bittersweet flavor and by itself is a refreshing hot weather drink. Combined with a variety of ingredients, it enhances flavors and adds zest.

Citric Tonic

¼ cup orange juice
tonic water
crushed ice

Fill glass one third full of crushed ice. Add juice and fill with tonic. ALTERNATIVES: Use lemon or lime juice in place of orange juice.

Cafe Tonic

½ cup iced coffee (see p. 71)
1 tbsp. sugar syrup (see p. 5)
tonic water
ice cubes

Place 3-4 ice cubes in tall glass. Add coffee and syrup. Fill with tonic and stir gently.

Iced Tea Tonic

½ cup iced tea (see pg. 80)
1 tbsp. sugar syrup (see p. 5)
tonic water
ice cubes

Place 3-4 ice cubes in tall glass. Add tea and syrup. Fill with tonic and stir gently.

Tonic Solo

twist of lemon or slice of lime
tonic water
crushed ice

Fill tall glass one third full of ice. Add lemon or lime and fill with tonic water.

Tonic Refresher

tonic water
slice of unpeeled cucumber
ice cubes

Fill glass half full of ice. Add cucumber slice and fill with tonic water.

Bitter lemon is the top of the line in mixes. Whole lemons are added to carbonated water and quinine. This mix can truly stand alone, serving it over ice, or mixed as in the following recipes.

Brisk Rose

1½ tbsp. grenadine
bitter lemon
crushed ice

Fill tall glass half full of ice. Add grenadine and fill with bitter lemon.

Cranberry Bitter

½ cup cranberry juice
½ cup bitter lemon
crushed ice

Fill tall glass one third full of crushed ice. Add cranberry juice and bitter lemon and stir gently to combine.

Mint Bint

2½ tbsp. mint syrup
bitter lemon
crushed ice
sprig of fresh mint

Fill tall glass half full of crushed ice. Add mint syrup and bitter lemon and stir gently. Garnish with mint.

Frosted Herb Nectar

¼ cup hot water
½ tsp. dried tarragon leaves
⅓ cup peach nectar
⅓ cup pineapple juice
bitter lemon
ice cubes

Pour boiling water over tarragon leaves and steep for 5 minutes. Strain and chill. Place 3-4 ice cubes in tall glass and add herbed brew, peach nectar and pineapple juice. Fill with bitter lemon and stir gently.

Pineapple Frost

⅔ cup pineapple juice
1/8 tsp. mint extract
bitter lemon
ice cubes

Place 3-4 ice cubes in tall glass. Add pineapple juice and extract. Fill with bitter lemon. Garnish with fresh mint if desired.

Bitter Lemon Twist

twist of lemon peel
several dashes of bitters
bitter lemon
cracked ice

Fill tall glass half full of crushed ice. Add ingredients, filling glass with bitter lemon. Stir gently.

Colas often stand alone. Try one of the following for a snazzy drink.

Root beer can stand alone too, but try this surprising variation.

Cola Swirl

2   tsp. lemon juice
1/8 tsp. peppermint
slice of lemon
cola
mint candy stick
ice cubes

Place 3-4 ice cubes in tall glass. Add lemon juice and extract. Fill with cola. Garnish with lemon slice, using candy stick as muddler.

Cola Coda

3   tbsp. crushed pineapple
½   tsp. lime juice
cola
curry powder
ice cubes

Fill tall glass half full of ice. Add pineapple and lime juice. Fill with cola and stir gently. Sprinkle lightly with curry powder. A little goes a long way.

Black and White

cola
milk
ice cubes

Place 3-4 ice cubes in tall glass. Fill three-fourths full of cola. Fill with milk and stir gently.

Root Beer Twist

2   tsp. lime juice
twist of lime rind
root beer
ice cubes

Place 3-4 ice cubes in tall glass. Add lime juice and rind. Fill with root beer and stir gently.

...or a no-fizz drink

Easily prepared non-carbonated drinks.

A natural follow up to the previous chapter are these non-carbonated drinks to be mixed one at a time. Some are old familiar drinks with a few new twists such as lemonade with lime juice and strawberries added. Also, you'll discover egg drinks like the Prairie Popper and some scrumptious versions of chocolate milk. Try these and don't miss the pleasure of some off beat flavors such as "Apricot Pleasure" or "Pineapple Rouge." Never be intimidated by a peculiar ingredient. You may think you don't like buttermilk but try a shot of "Buttermilk Nectar." It could become your fountain of youth.

Lemonade Plain

juice of 1 lemon
1 tbsp. sugar syrup (see p. 5)
½ cup water
crushed ice

Combine lemon juice, sugar syrup and water. Fill a tall glass half full of crushed ice and pour mixture over it. Garnish with mint if desired.
FANCY ALTERNATIVES:
in place of lemon juice:
1 lemon and 1 orange
1 lime and 1 orange
1 lime and ½ lemon
1 lime and 4 kumquats

Lemon Sour

1 tbsp. lemon juice
1 tbsp. lime juice
1 tbsp. sugar
¾ cup cold water
lemon slice
maraschino cherry

Combine ingredients, stirring to dissolve sugar. Serve over ice in tall glass. Garnish with lemon slice and cherry.

Lemon Daisy

juice of 1 lemon
1½ tbsp. grenadine
½ cup water
crushed ice

Fill tall glass half full of cracked ice. Combine other ingredients and pour over ice.
ALTERNATIVE: To the above add one of the following:
¼ cup slightly crushed red
    raspberries
¼ cup fresh or canned pineapple
¼ cup crushed strawberries
¼ cup ripe cherries (remove pits)
Garnish with a cherry
Use raspberry syrup in place of
    grenadine.

Gulf Crush

3 tbsp. frozen orange concentrate
½ cup water
crushed ice

Combine ingredients and serve.
ALTERNATIVE: Use limeade concentrate in place of orange.

Tropical Orange Crush

⅔ cup orange juice
1 ring of pineapple
1 tsp. lemon juice
2-3 ice cubes with mint sprig (see ices)

Blend orange juice, pineapple and lemon juice for 30 seconds. Serve over cubes in tall glass. Garnish with mint if desired.

Lime Slush

4 tbsp. frozen limeade
⅔ concentrate
3 cups crushed ice
    drops mint extract

Blend on high speed for a few seconds until snow forms. Garnish with a cherry if desired.
ALTERNATIVES: Use orange concentrate and garnish with orange slices.

Crackling Fruitail

1 part lime juice
4 parts sweet juice from any
    canned fruit (pear, peach, etc.)
cracked ice

Fill glass half full of cracked ice. Combine ingredients and pour over ice. Garnish as desired.

Pineapple Snow

3 tbsp. pineapple (fresh or canned)
1 tbsp. lime juice
1½ tsp. sugar
½ cup cracked ice

Combine ingredients and blend on high for a few seconds. Serve over ice. Garnish with a slice of lime if desired.

Pineapple Rouge

⅔ cup canned pineapple juice
½ tsp. sugar
2 tbsp. cream
dash of grenadine
crushed ice

Combine pineapple juice, sugar, cream and grenadine. Stir to dissolve sugar. Pour over ice and serve. Garnish as desired.

Hawaiian Haste

⅓ cup pineapple juice
juice of ½ lemon
¼ tsp. brown sugar
crushed ice

Shake all ingredients and serve.

Purple Stem

3 tbsp. grape concentrate
1 tbsp. sugar
crushed ice

Fill glass half full of ice. Combine other ingredients and pour over ice.

Rising Moon

½ cup grape juice
juice of 1 lime
peel of ½ lime

Squeeze lime and add juice to grape juice. Pour over ice to serve, adding lime peel. Garnish with 2-3 halved kumquats.

Orange Twist

½ cup orange juice
1 tbsp. raspberry syrup
crushed ice

Combine ingredients and serve over crushed ice. Garnish with slices of lemon or lime.
ALTERNATIVES: Use other fruit syrups in place of raspberry syrup.

Apricot Pleasure

4 dried apricot halves
¾ cup cold unsweetened grapefruit juice
1 tsp. honey
crushed ice

Soak apricots until soft, then dice. Place apricots, grapefruit juice, honey in blender and process on high speed for few seconds. Serve over crushed ice in tall glass. Sprinkle with ginger if desired.

Rosy Lady

juice of 1 orange
1 tbsp. cherry syrup or grenadine
1 tsp. spicy sugar syrup (see below)
2 tsp. egg white
crushed ice

Shake all ingredients until frothy. Garnish with slice of orange. Serve.

Spicy Sugar Syrup

6 whole cloves
⅓ cup water
1 cup sugar
3 slices unpeeled lemon
3 slices unpeeled orange

Boil 5 minutes, cool. Strain, cover and store in refrigerator.

Sweet Charity

2 tbsp. lime juice
½ cup grape juice
crushed ice

Fill glass one third full of crushed ice. Pour juices over ice and serve. ALTERNATIVE: Use any other sweet fruit juice in place of grape juice.

Lime Beauty

juice of ½ lime
1 egg white, unbeaten
2 dashes bitters
2 tsp. sugar syrup (see pg. 5)
ice cubes

Shake all ingredients and strain into glass.

Herbed Pineapple Froth

⅓ cup water
1 tsp. marjoram
¾ cup pineapple juice
1 tsp. egg white, unbeaten
ice cubes

Bring water to boil. Pour over marjoram and steep for 5 minutes. Cool and strain. Shake other ingredients until frothy. Strain, add herbed brew, and serve.

Sunrise Cocktail

juice of 1 orange
1 tsp. grenadine
1 tsp. egg white, unbeaten
½ cup crushed ice

Shake and strain. Serve.

Crackling Grape

⅓ cup grape juice
1 tbsp. lime juice
1 tsp. egg white, unbeaten
cracked ice

Fill glass half full of ice. Shake other ingredients and pour over ice and serve.

Bitter Lime

juice of ½ large lime
1 egg white, unbeaten
3 dashes bitters

Shake vigorously with ice until light and frothy. Strain and serve.

Pink Lemorange

⅔ cup orange juice
¼ cup lemon juice
1 tsp. grenadine
1 tsp. egg yolk, unbeaten
crushed ice

Shake thoroughly with crushed ice. Serve, adding more ice if desired.

Golden Lemon Break

juice of 1 lemon
2 egg yolks, unbeaten
1 tsp powdered sugar
¾ cup water

Shake and strain. Garnish with orange slice or cherry.
ALTERNATIVE: Use egg white and soda water for a fluffier, lighter drink.

Orange Derby

3 tbsp. frozen orange concentrate
½ tsp. lemon juice
2 tsp. egg white, unbeaten
¼ cup cracked ice
½ tsp. orange rind

Shake vigorously with ice until light and frothy. Serve, adding more ice if desired.

Egg Nog

1 egg
2 tsp. sugar
1/8 tsp. salt
¼ tsp. vanilla
1 cup milk

Beat egg, sugar and salt. Add milk and vanilla. Serve. Garnish with a sprinkle of nutmeg.

Cider Nog

1 egg
1 tsp. sugar
½ cup crushed ice
¾ cup cider

Shake egg, sugar and ice. Strain and add cider. Garnish with a sprinkle of nutmeg.

Orange Nog

2½ tbsp. frozen orange concentrate
¾ cup milk
1 egg

Blend ingredients and serve.

Prairie Popper

Drink this one without breaking the yolk.
1 egg yolk
1 tsp. worcestershire sauce
4 dashes vinegar
tabasco to taste
pinch of salt and pepper

Mix all ingredients in a glass except the yolk. Slip yolk into glass without breaking. Serve.
ALTERNATIVES: Make as above using whole egg and 1½ tsp. ketchup.

Rose Petal

¾ cup cold milk
1 tbsp. grenadine

Pour milk and grenadine over ice. Stir and serve.

Berry Shake

1 cup cold milk
2 tbsp. strawberry preserves
1 scoop vanilla ice cream

Combine preserves and milk and shake until well mixed. Add ice cream and serve.
ALTERNATIVES: Other fruit preserves may also be used.

Orange Milk

1 cup milk
peel of 1 orange
sugar

Heat milk to boiling point and pour over orange peel in glass or earthenware teapot. Cover and steep for 15 minutes. Remove peel and chill before serving. Add sugar to taste.

Chocolate Milk

1 cup milk
3 tbsp. chocolate syrup

Combine and serve.

Iced Chocolate Milk

1 cup milk
3 tbsp. chocolate syrup
crushed ice

Combine milk and syrup and pour over crushed ice. Top with whipped cream.

Chocolate Mountain High

¾ cup cold milk
3 tbsp. chocolate syrup
1 tsp. sugar
1 scoop vanilla ice cream

Blend and serve. Garnish with whipped cream.

Orange Yogurt

2 tbsp. frozen orange concentrate
½ cup plain yogurt

Blend on high for a few seconds.
ALTERNATIVE: Use ¼ cup pineapple juice and ¼ cup yogurt.

Yogurt Puff

½ cup plain yogurt
½ cup cold milk
salt to taste

Beat milk and yogurt until smooth. Add salt. Serve over ice. Garnish with a sprinkle of dried mint or ground ginger.
ALTERNATIVES:
Use sugar and ground cardamon in place of salt. Omit garnish.
Make as above, seasoning with hot chili pepper. Omit garnish.

Buttermilk Nectar

½ cup very cold buttermilk
½ cup apricot nectar
sugar to taste

Combine above ingredients and serve.
ALTERNATIVE: Use ⅓ cup pineapple juice in place of apricot nectar.

Other individually mixed drinks are:
Clam-Up Cocktail 54
Clam Shake 54
Sparkling Tomato Cocktail 52

Take the punch out of the bowl

Refreshing year-round drinks and drink bases served in glasses or from a punch bowl.

Throw out the traditional image of punch in crystal bowls served only at dainty parties and receptions. In reality punches are pleasing combinations of two or more beverages with unlimited serving possibilities. Look up recipes using your favorite beverages to see what delicious punches can be made with them. Then, go on to discover new taste vistas. If you plan to serve a crowd, utilize the hints on punch bowls and garlands in the beginning of this book. If you have witnessed as many "after the party" punch bowl tables as I have, this chapter is still for you. To prevent the litter of soaked napkins and splotched table linens the instructions in this chapter are written so you can also mix and serve these drinks individually. Large commercial-sized mayonnaise jars are useful for mixing and storing large batches. Superior flavors will develop if you mix and refrigerate the non-carbonated ingredients an hour before serving. Add carbonated beverages just before serving for a sparkling fresh drink.

Tropical Treat

1　pkg. strawberry flavored soft
　　drink mix
2　quarts water
½　cup sugar
3　cups pineapple juice
½　(6 oz. size) can frozen lemon
　　juice
16 oz. ginger ale or lemon-lime
carbonated beverage

Combine soft drink mix with sugar
and water and stir to dissolve. Add
pineapple juice and lemon concentrate. Just before serving add ginger ale. Garnish with fresh pineapple chunks. Makes 16 (8 oz.) servings. For individual servings combine in the following proportions — 8 parts fruit mix: 1 part
ginger ale.

Sparkling Fruit Drink

½　cup sugar
½　cup water
½　cup grapefruit juice
¼　cup orange juice
¼　cup grenadine
16 oz. ginger ale

Boil sugar and water for 8 minutes.
Cool and add fruit juices and grenadine. Gently add ginger ale and
serve immediately. Makes 4 (8 oz.)
servings or 8 (4 oz.) punch size
servings. For individual servings
combine in the following proportions — 1 part fruit syrup: 1 part
ginger ale.

Pineapple Cherry Bubble

⅓　cup sugar
1　cup lemon juice
1　cup cherry juice (not maras-
　　chino juice)
2　cups pineapple juice
16 oz. ginger ale

Combine sugar with fruit juices
and stir to dissolve. Gently add
ginger ale and serve immediately.
Makes 8 (8 oz.) servings. For individual servings combine in the following proportions — 1 part fruit
mixture: 1 part ginger ale.

Orange Pineapple Pleasure

1　(3 oz.) pkg. orange flavored
　　gelatin
1　cup boiling water
1　(6 oz.) can frozen pineapple
　　concentrate
3　(6 oz.) cans water
4　cups apple juice
1　(28 oz.) bottle ginger ale

Pour hot water over gelatin and stir
to dissolve. Add fruit juices and
cold water. Mix. Gently add ginger
ale and serve immediately. Makes
12 (8 oz.) servings. For individual
servings combine in the following
proportions — 3 parts fruit juice
mixture: 1 part ginger ale.

Orange Jubilee

1　(6 oz.) can frozen orange
　　concentrate
¼　cup light corn syrup
1　(28 oz.) bottle ginger ale

Combine concentrate and syrup
and mix until smooth. Gently add
ginger ale and serve immediately.
Makes 6 (6 oz.) servings. For individual servings combine in the following proportions — 1 part fruit
juice mixture: 3½ parts ginger ale.

Ginger Ale Gala

1 cup pineapple juice
1 (12 oz.) can frozen orange concentrate
⅓ cup lemon juice
¼ cup maraschino cherry juice
2 qt. ginger ale

Combine first four ingredients and stir to dissolve orange concentrate. Add ginger ale just before serving. Makes 7 (8 oz.) servings. For individual servings, combine in the following proportions — 1 part fruit mixture: 2 parts ginger ale.

Great Grape

2½ cups pineapple juice
2½ cups orange juice
2½ cups grape juice
2 tbsp. lemon juice
16 oz. ginger ale

Combine fruit juices. Gently add ginger ale and serve immediately. Makes 10 (8 oz.) servings. For individual servings, combine in the following proportions — 4 parts fruit mixture: 1 part ginger ale.

Pineapple Slush

3 cups pineapple juice
1 quart lemon or pineapple sherbet
1 (28 oz.) bottle ginger ale

Mix juice and sherbet until smooth. Gently add ginger ale and serve. Makes 10 (8 oz.) servings or 20 (4 oz.) punch size servings. For individual servings combine in the following proportions — 2 parts sherbet fruit mixture: 1 part ginger ale.

Rosied Ale

1 (46 oz.) can tropical fruit punch
¼ cup instant tea powder
¼ cup lemon juice
1 (26 oz.) bottle ginger ale

Combine punch, powder and lemon juice. Stir to dissolve. Add ginger ale and serve immediately. Garnish with fruited ice cubes if desired. Makes 10 (8 oz.) servings. For individual servings combine in the following proportions — 2 parts fruit mixture: 1 part ginger ale.

Celebration Frost

1 (6 oz.) can frozen lemonade concentrate
1 (6 oz.) can frozen orange juice concentrate
1 (6 oz.) can frozen pineapple juice concentrate
2 quarts water
1½ cups apricot nectar
½ cup lemon juice
1 quart lemon sherbet
2 (28 oz.) bottles ginger ale

Combine concentrates with water, nectar and lemon juice. Mix until smooth. Add sherbet just before serving. Gently add ginger ale. Serve immediately. Makes 24 (8 oz.) servings or 48 (4 oz.) punch size servings. For individual servings combine in the following proportions — 4 parts fruit mixture: 1 part sherbet: 2 parts ginger ale.

Pink Curry Cup

2 cups buttermilk
1 (8 oz.) can tomato sauce
1 cucumber, finely chopped
1 tsp. Worchestershire sauce
½ tsp. curry powder

Mix all ingredients until well blended. Garnish with slice of green pepper or unpeeled cucumber slice. Makes 6 (5 oz.) servings.

Lime Lighter

2 pkg. lime flavored soft drink mix
1 cup sugar
8 cups water
1 (46 oz.) can unsweetened pineapple juice
16 oz. ginger ale

Mix drink powder with sugar and water and stir to dissolve. Add pineapple juice and stir to mix. Gently add ginger ale and serve immediately. Makes 15 (8 oz.) servings or 30 (4 oz.) punch size servings. For individual servings combine in the following proportions — 6 parts fruit mixture: 1 part ginger ale.

Super Orange

½ (6 oz.) can frozen orange concentrate
½ cup water
½ cup milk
¼ cup sugar
½ tsp. vanilla
5-6 ice cubes

Put ingredients in blender and blend on low speed for 30 seconds. Makes 3 (8 oz.) servings.

Orange Lemonale

1 cup cold water
¾ cup sugar
1 cup lemon juice
1 cup orange juice
1 (28 oz.) bottle ginger ale

Combine sugar with water and fruit juices. Stir to dissolve. Add ginger ale and serve immediately. Garnish with a twist of lemon or a slice of orange. Makes 6 (8 oz.) servings or 12 (4 oz.) punch size servings. For individual servings combine in the following proportions — 1 part fruit mixture: 1 part ginger ale.

Grande Grape

2½ cups grape juice
1½ cups orange juice
2　(28 oz.) bottles ginger ale

Combine fruit juices. Gently add ginger ale and serve immediately. Makes 10 (9 oz.) servings. For individual servings, combine in the following proportions — 1 part fruit juice mixture: 2 parts ginger ale

Gingermint

1　(10 oz.) jar mint jelly
1½ cups water
3　cups unsweetened pineapple juice
½　cup lemon juice
2　(28 oz.) bottles ginger ale

Combine jelly and water, heat and stir until smooth. Cool. Add fruit juices. Gently add ginger ale and serve immediately. Makes 10 (10 oz.) servings. For individual servings combine in the following proportions — 1 part fruit syrup: 1 part ginger ale.

Lemon Sparkle

2　(6 oz.) cans frozen lemonade concentrate
2　(6 oz.) cans frozen pineapple concentrate
3　(6 oz.) cans water
2　(28 oz.) bottles ginger ale
14 oz. carbonated water

Mix fruit concentrates and water until smooth. Add carbonated beverages and serve immediately. Garnish with a slice of lemon or fresh pineapple. Makes 14 (8 oz.) servings or 28 (4 oz.) punch size servings. For individual servings combine in the following proportions — 3 parts fruit mixture: 2 parts ginger ale: 1 part carbonated water.

Betsey Cider

1   cup cider
½   cup orange juice
3   tbsp. lemon juice
2   egg whites, unbeaten
1   tsp. powdered sugar
½   cup crushed ice

Put all ingredients in blender and mix on high speed until foamy. Garnish with a sprinkle of nutmeg. Makes 4 (5 oz.) servings.

Mint Lemonale

6   cups sugar
4   cups water
1   cup mint leaves
4   cups lemon juice
2   cups ice water
2   (28 oz.) bottles ginger ale

Combine sugar and water and boil for 5 minutes. Add mint and lemon juice and cool. Strain and add ice water. Gently add ginger ale and serve immediately. Garnish with sprig of fresh mint. Makes 18 (8 oz.) servings or 36 (4 oz.) servings. For individual servings combine in the following proportions — 2 parts fruit syrup: 3 parts ginger ale

Fruit Sparkle

1   cup sugar
1   quart water
½   cup mint leaves
1   cup lemon juice
1   quart orange juice
1   cup pineapple juice
1   (28 oz.) bottle ginger ale

Makes 12 (8 oz.) servings or 24 (4 oz.) punch size servings. Simmer sugar, water and mint leaves for 10 minutes. Chill and strain. Add fruit juices and stir. Add ginger ale and serve immediately. For individual servings combine in the following proportions — 2 parts fruit syrup mixture: 1 part ginger ale.

Ciderbelle

4   cups cider
1⅓ cups pineapple juice
⅔   cup orange juice
⅓   cup lemon juice

Mix all ingredients until well combined. Chill and serve. Garnish with fresh mint leaves. Makes 6 (8 oz.) servings.

Sweet 'n Tart Cubes

1   pkg. raspberry flavored soft drink mix
½   cup sugar
4   cups unsweetened pineapple juice
lemon-lime carbonated beverage

Combine drink mix, sugar and pineapple juice and stir until dissolved. Freeze. To serve place 3-4 cubes in tall glass and fill with lemon-lime carbonated beverage. Makes 2-3 trays of cubes.

Raspberry Orange Fizz

1   pkg. raspberry flavored soft drink mix
2   quarts water
½   cup sugar
1   (6 oz.) can frozen orange juice
1   (28 oz.) bottle lemon-lime carbonated beverage

Combine drink mix with water and sugar. Stir to dissolve. Add orange juice and mix. Gently add ginger ale and serve immediately. Makes 12 (8 oz.) servings. For individual servings, combine in the following proportions — 3 parts fruit mix: 1 part lemon-lime carbonated beverage (approx.)

Orange Delight

orange juice
lemon-lime carbonated beverage or ginger ale

Fill glass(es) half full of ice and pour equal parts juice and carbonated beverage over and serve immediately. Garnish with a fresh slice of citrus fruit.
HINT: For picnics, freeze orange juice in cubes and carry in ice bucket. Pour carbonated beverage over and serve.

Twisted Apricot Nectar

1   **(6 oz.) can frozen lemonade**
    concentrate
3   **(6 oz.) cans water**
1½ **tbsp. instant tea**
¼   **cup sugar**
1½ **cups apricot nectar**
1   **(28 oz.) bottle ginger ale**

Combine lemon concentrate with water. Add tea, sugar, nectar, and stir to dissolve. Add ginger ale and serve immediately. Makes 8 (8 oz.) servings. For individual servings combine in the following proportions — 2 parts fruit juice mixture: 1 part ginger ale.

Sparkling Nectar

1⅓ **cup tea**
2   **tbsp. sugar**
⅓   **cup lemon juice**
⅔   **cup orange juice**
1½ **cup apricot nectar**
1   **cup ginger ale**

Mix tea, sugar and fruit juice until sugar is dissolved. Gently add ginger ale and serve immediately. Makes 4 (10 oz.) servings or 8 (5 oz.) servings. For individual servings combine in the following proportions — 4 parts fruit mixture: 1 part ginger ale.

Lemon Horizon

½   **cup lemon juice**
¼   **cup lime juice**
½   **cup granulated sugar**
½   **cup chopped ice**
1¼ **cups club soda**

Put all ingredients in blender and mix at high speed for 30 seconds. Serve immediately. Garnish with cherry. Makes 6 (4 oz.) servings. For individual servings combine in the following proportions 3 parts fruit mixture: 2 parts soda.

Frosted Orange Frappé

1   **tbsp. grated orange peel**
2   **cups boiling water**
1   **cup sugar**
1   **cup orange juice**
2   **tbsp. lemon juice**
ginger ale or lemon-lime carbonated beverage

Stir together water, sugar and peel until sugar dissolves. Add fruit juices and freeze until firm. Remove from freezer and beat until smooth and fluffy. Return to freezer. To serve, scoop frappé into glasses and fill with ginger ale or lemon-lime carbonated beverage. Serve immediately. Garnish with mint if desired. Makes slightly more than a quart of freezer mixture.

Rosy Slush

½ **cup sugar**
1 **cup water**
1 **cup orange juice**
1 **cup lemon juice**
2 **tbsp. grenadine**
ginger ale

Combine sugar with water, juices and grenadine. Stir to dissolve sugar. Freeze into cubes. When serving, place 3-4 cubes in a tall glass and fill with ginger ale. Makes slightly more than 2 trays of cubes.

Fruited Julep

1½ **cups grape juice**
1½ **cups grape fruit juice**
1½ **cups cider**
1 **(28 oz.) bottle ginger ale**

Mix fruit juices and add ginger ale just before serving. Garnish with fresh mint. Serve in tall frosted glasses. Makes 8 (8 oz.) servings. For individual servings combine in the following proportions — approx. 3 parts fruit juice mixture: 2 parts ginger ale.

Fruit Frolic

1 **(46 oz.) can tropical fruit punch**
1 **(28 oz.) bottle soda water**
1 **(28 oz.) bottle lemon sour**

Gently combine all ingredients and serve immediately. Garnish with fresh fruit chunks. Makes 15 (8 oz.) servings or 30 (4 oz.) punch size servings. For individual servings combine in the following proportions — 2 parts tropical punch: 1 part lemon sour: 1 part soda water.

Fabulous Fizz

3 **(6 oz.) cans frozen lemonade concentrate**
2 **cups light corn syrup**
2 **(28 oz.) bottles raspberry or cherry carbonated beverage**
1 **(28 oz.) bottle ginger ale**

Combine lemonade concentrate and syrup. Add carbonated beverages and serve over ice immediately. Makes 14 (8 oz.) servings or 28 (4 oz.) punch size servings. For individual servings combine in the following proportions — 1 part lemonade syrup: 2 parts cherry carbonated beverage: 1 part ginger ale (approx.).

Almond Refresher

1   (3 oz.) pkg. lime flavored gelatin
1   cup hot water
⅓   cup lime juice
2   (6 oz.) cans frozen limeade concentrate
½   tsp. almond extract
1   quart lime sherbet
½   cup lemon-lime carbonated beverage

Mix gelatin and water until dissolved. Add lime juice, concentrate and extract. Just before serving, add scoops of sherbet and carbonated beverage. Makes 8 (8 oz.) servings or 16 (4 oz.) servings. For individual servings combine in the following proportions — 1 part fruit juice mixture: 1 part sherbet plus a touch of carbonated beverage.

Apricot Orange Drink

3   cups apricot nectar
1½ cups orange juice
¾   cup lemon juice
4   cups cider

Combine all ingredients and refrigerate before serving. Garnish with fresh lemon slices. Makes 9 (8 oz.) servings.

Black Cherry Charge

1   (6 oz.) can frozen lemonade concentrate
1½ (6 oz.) cans water
½   cup grenadine
1   (28 oz.) bottle black cherry soda
1   (28 oz.) bottle carbonated water

Combine lemonade concentrate, water and grenadine. Stir until smooth. Gently add soda and carbonated water and serve. Garnish with lime slices or maraschino cherry. Makes 9 (8 oz.) servings or approx. 18 (4 oz.) servings. For individual servings combine in the following proportions — 1 part lemonade mixture: 1½ parts cherry soda: 1½ parts soda water.

Reformation Tea

2 quarts strong tea, cooled
1 (6 oz.) can frozen orange juice concentrate
1 (6 oz.) can frozen grape juice concentrate
1 (6 oz.) can frozen lemonade concentrate
1 (28 oz.) bottle ginger ale

Combine all ingredients except ginger ale and stir until smooth. Just before serving, gently add ginger ale. Garnish with thin slices of orange or lemon. Makes 15 (8 oz.) servings. For individual servings combine in the following proportions — 2½ parts fruited tea mixture: 1 part ginger ale.

Frosty Lady

1 cup lime juice
1 cup orange juice
¾ cup granulated sugar
1½ tsp. cherry juice
dashes of bitters to taste

Put all ingredients in blender and blend at medium speed for about 1 minute. Or put ingredients in covered jar and shake until frothy. Garnish with cherries or orange and lime slices. Makes four 6 oz. servings.

Summer Jubilee

1 cup sugar
6 cups hot water
1 (6 oz.) can lemonade concentrate
1 cup strong black tea
1 cup orange juice
4 cups cranberry cocktail juice
1½ cups apple juice

Dissolve sugar in water. Cool. Add other ingredients. Refrigerate for a few hours to enhance flavor. Makes 15 (8 oz.) servings or 30 (4 oz.) punch size servings.

Fruit Supreme

1 **(6 oz.) can frozen orange juice**
3 **(6 oz.) cans water**
1 **(6 oz.) can frozen lemonade concentrate**
3 **(6 oz.) cans water**
1½ **cups apricot nectar**
2 **cups pineapple juice**

Combine frozen concentrates with water and mix until smooth. Add nectar and pineapple juice and mix. Chill. Garnish with fresh fruit. Makes 10 (8 oz.) servings or 20 (4 oz.) punch size servings.

Lemonade Rose

1 **(12 oz.) can frozen lemonade concentrate**
1 **(12 oz.) can water**
1 **(28 oz.) bottle strawberry soda**

Combine concentrate and water and stir until smooth. Add strawberry soda and serve immediately. Garnish with lemon slices. Makes 6 (8 oz.) servings. For individual servings, combine in the following proportions — 1 part lemonade mixture: 1 part strawberry soda.

Fruited Tea Punch

2 **quarts water**
¾ **cup instant tea**
1 **(6 oz.) can frozen limeade concentrate**
1 **(6 oz.) can frozen lemonade concentrate**
1 **(6 oz.) can frozen pineapple juice concentrate**
2 **cups cranberry juice cocktail**
2 **cups ginger ale**

Combine tea and water stirring until dissolved. Add fruit concentrates and cranberry cocktail. Stir until smooth. Just before serving, add ginger ale and serve over ice. Garnish with slice of lemon or lime or chunk of pineapple. Makes 14 (8 oz.) or 28 (4 oz.) punch size servings.

Lemonade Royale

juice of 2 lemons
¼ **cup sugar**
1⅓ **cup grape juice**
2 **cups ice water**

Dissolve sugar in lemon juice. Add grape juice and water. Chill and serve. Makes 4 (8 oz.) servings.

Start with fresh fruit

Mix fun into a cool drink with
anything from a lemon to a
watermelon

Pineapple Surprise

3½ cups apple juice
3½ cups pineapple juice
¼ cup maraschino cherry juice
¼ tsp. almond extract

Combine all ingredients. Chill and
serve. Garnish with maraschino
cherry and sprig of mint. Makes 9
(6 oz.) servings.

Pineapple Chunk

6 cups pineapple juice
1½ cups orange juice
¾ cup lemon juice
3 tbsp. lime juice
1 cup sugar
2 (28 oz.) bottle ginger ale
1 (28 oz.) bottle carbonated water

Combine fruit juices and stir to
dissolve sugar. Gently add ginger
ale and soda. Serve immediately.
Garnish with chunks of canned or
fresh pineapple. Makes 20 (8 oz.)
servings or 40 (4 oz.) punch size
servings. For individual servings,
combine in the following proportions — 3 parts fruit mixture: 2
parts ginger ale: 1 part soda water.

Congeniality Party Punch

2 quarts strong tea, cooled
1 quart orange juice
6 cups grape juice
2 cups lemon juice
1 cup sugar
1 quart cold water
1 (28 oz.) bottle ginger ale

Combine tea, fruit juices, sugar
and water. Stir to dissolve sugar.
Just before serving, gently add ginger ale. Makes 32 (8 oz.) servings.
For individual servings combine in
the following proportions — 6
parts tea mixture: 1 part ginger
ale.

Grape Gala

2½ cups apple juice
3½ cups grape juice
2 tbsp. lime juice
½ tsp. nutmeg

Combine fruit juices and nutmeg.
Chill and serve. Garnish with slices
of fresh lime. Makes 8 (6 oz.)
servings.

July Julep

¼ cup orange juice
¼ cup grape juice
few grains of salt
½ cup ice water
¼ cup lemon juice
¼ cup sugar

Combine in blender at low speed
for 30 seconds. Or put in covered
jar and shake. Serve over crushed
ice in tall frosted glasses. Garnish
with mint sprigs. Makes 2 (6 oz.)
servings.

Start with fresh fruit

Mix the ultimate fruit drink with anything from a banana to a persimmon.

What is more refreshing than an icy cold drink filled with your favorite fruit? Here are the drinks made with fresh, canned or frozen fruits. Some are left whole as in "Raspberry Mint Twist," others are blended as in "Coffee Peach Shake." Fruits mashed and frozen into slushes are easy to make and store indefinitely in your freezer. These drinks are a treat on a hot afternoon or make marvelous desserts when accompanied by a tray of light bars or cookies. These are but a sampling of the wide variety of fruit drinks. Mix them; substitute as you choose; create your own ultimate fruit drink. If you don't have on hand a crate of exotic fruit from Madagascar, this chapter will get you started with fruits you *do* have in your own kitchen.

Raspberry Mint Twist

⅓ cup sugar
½ cup mint leaves (lightly packed)
1 cup boiling water
1 (10 oz.) package frozen red raspberries
1 (6 oz.) can frozen lemonade concentrate

Add sugar and mint leaves to boiling water and simmer 5 minutes. Strain. Add raspberries and lemonade concentrate, stir to thaw. Add 2 cups cold water. Serve over ice. Garnish with fresh raspberries and mint leaves. Makes 6 (6 oz.) servings.

Raspberry Rag

1 (10 oz.) pkg. frozen raspberries
2½ cups cold milk
2 tsp. sugar
1 tsp. lemon juice

Blend and serve. Makes 4 (8 oz.) servings.

Rhubarb Refresher

4 cups rhubarb (cut into 1" pieces)
¾ cup water
3 cups sugar
⅔ cup orange juice
3 tbsp. lemon juice
2 (28 oz.) bottles ginger ale

Cook rhubarb and sugar in water until fruit softens. Put through food mill. Add orange and lemon juice. Stir to mix. Chill. Pour ½ cup juice mixture over ice. Fill remainder of glass with ginger ale. Serve immediately. Makes 10 (6 oz.) servings.

GROW YOUR OWN MINT in a kitchen herb garden. Plant it from seeds or make cuttings from already established plants and root in water. Grow this herb in a clay pot near a sunny window and you will be able to snip off fresh mint as needed.

Rhubarb Sparkler

4 cups fresh rhubarb (cut into 1" pieces)
2 cups water
3 cups sugar
1 cup pineapple juice
¾ cup lemon juice
1 (28 oz.) bottle ginger ale

Put rhubarb into sauce pan and add water to cover. Cook until soft and set aside. Mix sugar and water and cook for 10 minutes to make syrup. Combine with rhubarb and add pineapple and lemon juice. Just before serving, add ginger ale. Makes 1 gallon or 16 (8 oz.) servings.

Rhubarb Royale

6 cups tea
6 cups rhubarb (cut into ½" pieces)
1½ cups sugar

Combine ingredients and cook until rhubarb is tender.

Strain and serve over ice. Garnish with a twist of lemon. Makes 12 (8 oz.) servings.

Peachy Freeze

¾ cup cold milk
¾ cup chilled peaches
¼ tsp. salt
3 drops almond extract
½ cup vanilla ice cream

Blend milk, peaches, salt and almond extract until smooth. Add ice cream and blend until smooth. Makes 2 (8 oz.) servings.

Peach Starter

Try this for breakfast with a toasted English muffin.
2 peaches
2 eggs
¼ tsp. salt
2 tbsp. frozen orange concentrate
½ cup milk

Blend all ingredients until smooth and serve immediately. Makes 2 (8 oz.) servings.

Coffee Peach Shake

1 (1 lb.) can sliced cling peaches
2 tsp. instant coffee
¼ cup water
1 cup light cream
1 cup ice cream

Blend peaches, coffee, water and cream on high speed until smooth. Add ice cream, a chunk at a time. Makes 4 servings.

Peach Pineapple Frappé

1 cup fresh peaches
¾ cup milk
¼ cup unsweetened pineapple juice
¼ cup sugar
¼ tsp. salt
1 pint vanilla ice cream

Blend peaches, milk, juice and sugar until smooth. Add ice cream and blend until soft. Makes 4 (8 oz.) servings.

Icy Peach Blend

2 cups milk
1 pint peach ice cream
1 (10 oz.) pkg. frozen sliced peaches, thawed
1/8 tsp. almond extract

Blend milk, 1 cup ice cream, fruit and extract until smooth. Pour into glasses and top with scoop of ice cream. Makes 4 (10 oz.) servings.

Pineapple Pleasure

2 cups cherry juice
2 lemons, sliced thin
1 orange, peeled and sliced
1 pineapple, peeled and cut into small chunks
2 tbsp. sugar
2 (16 oz. each) bottles lemon-lime carbonated beverage

Add orange and lemon slices to cherry juice. Add pineapple chunks and sugar and stir to dissolve sugar. Cover and refrigerate overnight. Just before serving add carbonated beverage. Makes 10 (8 oz.) servings or 20 punch-size servings.

Strawberries Afloat

1   **(6 oz.) can frozen lemonade concentrate**
2   **(6 oz.) cans water**
1   **(10 oz.) pkg. frozen strawberries**
1   **(28 oz.) bottle ginger ale**

Mix concentrate and water until smooth. Add partially thawed strawberries. Gently add ginger ale and serve. Makes 7 (8 oz.) servings or 14 (4 oz.) servings. For individual servings combine in the following proportions — 1 part fruit mixture: 1 part ginger ale.

Orange Blossom

¼ **cup sugar**
boiling water
juice of 5 oranges
juice of ½ lemon
1½ cups crushed ice
3   **cups very cold water**

Pour just enough boiling water over sugar to cover and stir to dissolve. Add other ingredients. Shake until thoroughly cold and serve. Garnish with orange peel. ALTERNATIVE: Omit the sugar water for a lower calorie drink.

Strawberry Frost

1 (10 oz.) pkg. frozen strawberries
1 (6 oz.) can frozen lemonade
  concentrate
1 (6 oz.) can water
1 pint vanilla ice cream
1 (7 oz.) bottle lemon-lime carbonated beverage

Blend strawberries, lemonade, water and ice cream until smooth. Gently add lemon-lime carbonated beverage and serve immediately. Makes 8 (5½ oz.) servings.

YOGURT, a digestion-enhancing, tasty milk product created by those hardworking little bacteria, Lactobacillus Bulgaris, will add zest and character to many a beverage. In Turkey and the Balkan countries, yogurt is regarded as the fountain of youth; longevity and good health are guaranteed to its regular users. How can you go wrong?

Pineapple Passion

½ cup lemon juice
rind of ½ lemon
½ cup light corn syrup
1 cup crushed pineapple (fresh or
  canned)
2½ cups buttermilk

Combine all ingredients in blender for 30 seconds. Serve chilled. Makes 4 (8 oz.) servings.

Strawberried Yogurt

2 cups yogurt
1 (10 oz.) pkg. frozen strawberries

Combine in blender. Makes 2 servings.

Orange Strawberry Alert

1 cup orange juice
1 (10 oz.) pkg. frozen strawberries
  partly thawed
1 egg
½ cup dry milk
½ cup cold water

Blend to smooth mixture. Garnish with orange twist or fresh strawberries. Makes 4 (6½ oz.) servings.

Strawberry Passion

¾ cup fresh strawberries
1¼ cups cold buttermilk
sugar to taste

Blend strawberries and buttermilk until smooth. Add sugar if desired. Makes 2 (8 oz.) servings.

Après Dinner Fruit Freeze

1 cup milk
1 banana
1 orange, peeled
1 strip orange peel rind
2 tsp. sugar
1/8 tsp. vanilla
pinch of salt

Blend all ingredients to liquefy.
Pour into freezer tray. Partially
freeze. Makes 2 (10 oz.) servings.

Fresh Fruit Shake

1 cup cold milk
¾ cup persimmon
⅓ cup powdered milk
2 tsp. sugar
1 tsp. vanilla extract
1 egg, raw

Peel and slice fruit. Blend all ingredients. Chill and serve. Makes 2 (9
oz.) servings.
ALTERNATIVE: Use other fruits
such as: apricots, bananas, cherries, peaches, pineapple,
strawberries.

Banana Slush I

4 cups sugar
6 cups water
1 (46 oz.) can pineapple juice
2 (12 oz.) cans frozen orange juice
concentrate
1 (12 oz.) can frozen lemonade
concentrate
5 bananas
2 (16 oz.) bottles lemon-lime carbonated beverage

Dissolve sugar in water. Add juices
and mix. Put bananas through
food mill and stir into juices.
Freeze. To serve, thaw to mush
stage (about 4 hours in refrigerator). Fill glassware half full of mixture and add lemon-lime carbonated beverage. Garnish with strawberries. Makes 6 quarts, 24 (8 oz.)
servings.

Icy Fruit Frappé

2¼ cups sugar
juice of 6 lemons, rind of 1
juice of 2 oranges, rind of 1
1 (10 oz.) pkg. frozen strawberries
6 cups hot water
3 bananas, mashed

Mix sugar, fruit juices, rind to combine. Mash and add strawberries and water. Stir in mashed bananas. Chill in freezer trays until thick. Beat 3 egg whites and fold into fruit mixture. Freeze. Makes 12 (8 oz.) servings.
ALTERNATIVE: Fill glass half full of Icy Fruit Frappé and add lemon-lime carbonated beverage.

For a wonderful fresh lemon flavor, squeeze juice from lemon and grate the colored part of the rind into juice. Place in tightly covered container and set in refrigerator over night. Strain before using if desired. Try this with limes and oranges also. Use only the oily, colored part of the rinds as the white pulpy part of any fruit will give fresh juices a bitter taste.

Banana Slush II

1 cup sugar
4 cups water
1 (46 oz.) can pineapple juice
2 (6 oz.) can frozen orange juice concentrate
½ cup lime juice
3-5 bananas
2 (16 oz.) bottles ginger ale

Mash bananas; add other ingredients except ginger ale. Mix until smooth. Freeze until firm. To serve, fill cup half full of mixture and add ginger ale to top. Makes approximately 3 quarts of frozen mixture.

Banana Frappé

2 bananas, cut into chunks
½ cup pineapple juice
1 tbsp. powdered sugar
3 tbsp. lime juice
6 ice cubes, broken

Place banana, pineapple juice, sugar, lime juice and 3 ice cubes in blender for 1 minute. Add other ice cubes and blend 1 more minute. Serve immediately. Makes 3 (8 oz.) servings.

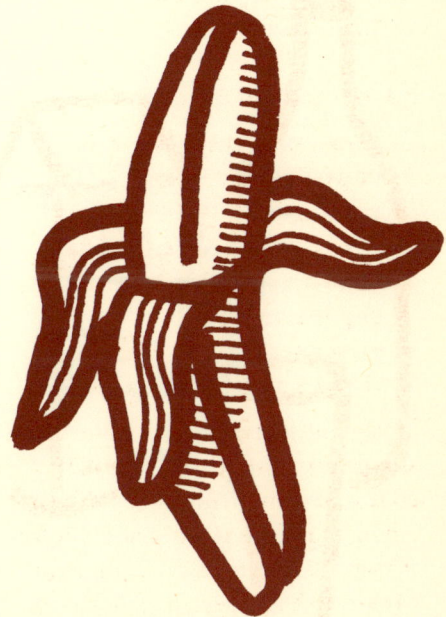

Banana Creme

1 **banana**
1 **egg**
1 **cup apple juice**

Put all ingredients in blender and mix on high speed until frothy. Makes 2-3 (6 oz.) servings.
ALTERNATIVE: Substitute another juice for the apple juice or use half apple juice and half another juice.

Raspberry Celebration

1 **(3 oz.) pkg. raspberry gelatin**
3 **cups boiling water**
¾ **cup sugar**
3 **cups cold water**
3 **cups orange juice**
¾ **cup lemon juice**
14 oz. **ginger ale**
1 **(10 oz.) pkg. frozen raspberries**

Mix gelatin and boiling water. Add sugar, mix until dissolved. Add cold water and fruit juices. Chill 2-3 hours. Before serving add slightly thawed raspberries and ginger ale. Makes 8 (8 oz.) servings or 16 (4 oz.) punch size servings.

Strawberry Melon Jubilee

1 **(46 oz.) can tropical fruit punch**
1 **(12 oz.) can frozen orange juice**
1 **cup cold water**
1 **(10 oz.) pkg. frozen strawberries**
1 **(10 oz.) pkg. frozen melon balls**

Combine punch, concentrate and water and stir until smooth. Add partially thawed strawberries and melon balls. Serve immediately Makes 8 (8 oz.) servings or 16 (4 oz.) punch size servings.

Pineapple Carrot Tippler

2 **cups unsweetened pineapple juice**
2 **medium carrots**
1 **(¼") slice of lemon**
1/8 tsp. **salt**
1 **cup ice**

Blend pineapple juice, carrots, lemon and salt to liquefy. Add ice and blend again to liquefy. Makes 4 (8 oz.) servings or 6 (5 oz.) servings.

Other recipes using fruit:

Toast the tomato

Bright, zingy complements for appetizers or meals.

Tomato drinks appeal to the eye as well as the palate. Serve them in chilled, clear glassware with imaginative garnishes like cucumber spears, lemon and lime slices, carrot sticks, celery stalks (with its foliage intact), green onions, olives or a slice of fresh mushroom. Spear a series of garnishes on a stir stick.

Subtle flavors will reveal themselves if these drinks are mixed ahead (except for those requiring carbonated beverages which should always be added just before serving). Offer guests a tray of suitable seasonings and let them season their own to taste. Include seasoned salts, freshly ground pepper, hot pepper sauce and fresh lemon slices.

Tomato drinks excel as appetizers or as luncheon beverages. For a light lunch, mix up Cauliflower Vinaigrette (page 54) and serve with a tomato drink and a basket of warm fresh bread.

Basiled Beef

1   can (10¾ oz.) beef broth
2   cups tomato juice
½   tsp. onion salt
1   tsp. Worcestershire sauce
1   tbsp. lemon juice

Combine ingredients. Serve over ice. Garnish with lemon wedge. Makes 4 (7 oz.) servings.

Mexi Tomato Garni

1   (46 oz.) can tomato juice
1   green pepper, chopped fine
1   onion, chopped fine
6   celery stalks, chopped fine
2   tbsp. cider vinegar
1   tbsp. sugar
5   bay leaves
15 whole peppers
10 cloves
2   tsp. salt
½   tsp. pepper

Combine all ingredients and heat to boiling. Lower heat and simmer for 10 minutes. Strain. Serve hot or cold. Makes 6 (8 oz.) servings.

Tomato Pow

1   (46 oz.) can tomato juice
2½ tbsp. prepared horseradish
1   tbsp. chopped onions
8   drops Tabasco sauce

Mix ingredients. Cover and refrigerate to allow flavors to blend. Makes 6 (8 oz.) servings.

Sparkling Tomato Cocktail

2   cups tomato juice
2   tbsp. lemon juice
2   tbsp. lime juice
1   can (12 oz.) lemon-lime carbonated beverage

Combine tomato juice with lemon and lime juices. Pour into 4 glasses. Slowly add lemon-lime carbonated beverage to each serving. Stir gently. Garnish with celery stick. Makes 4 (8 oz.) servings.
ALTERNATIVE: For individual servings, mix equal amounts of tomato juice and lemon-lime carbonated beverage. Add lemon and lime juice to taste.

Tomato Juice Cocktail

3½ cups tomato juice
2   slices of fresh lemon (with peel)
3   sprigs parsley
2   (½") strips green pepper
2   stalks celery (chopped in 1" pieces)
2   (½") slices cucumber (unpeeled)
½   tsp. Worcestershire sauce
¾   tsp. salt

Place ingredients in blender to liquefy. Serve over ice. Garnish with cucumber slice or celery stalk. Makes 4 (8 oz.) servings.

Seasoned Salt

1   cup salt
1   tbsp. paprika
1   tsp. mace
1   tsp. celery salt
1   tsp. thyme
1   tsp. oregano
1   tsp. garlic powder
1   tsp. onion powder
1   tsp. mustard

Make your own seasoned salt. Store in an airtight container. Gift Idea: Bring this as a hostess gift.

Herbed Consommé

3½ cups tomato juice
1 cup canned consommé
¼ tsp. marjoram
¼ tsp. thyme
dash of garlic powder
a few shakes of parsley

Combine ingredients. Chill and serve. Makes 6 (6 oz.) servings.

Tomato Toreador

3 green chilies (seeds removed)
1 can (18 oz.) tomato juice
½ tsp. salt

Place in blender to liquefy. Serve over ice. Garnish with lemon slice. Makes 3 (6 oz.) servings.
ALTERNATIVE: You may wish to add a crushed pinch of cumin to this drink.

CHILI PEPPERS are milder if seeds are removed. Green chilies will turn red if they are allowed to ripen and mature.

Day Break Juicer

1 cup tomato juice
1 cup grapefruit juice
½ tsp. Worcestershire sauce

Combine ingredients and serve over ice. Makes 2 (8 oz.) servings.

Celeried Tomato

4 cups tomato juice
¾ cup celery juice
1/8 tsp celery seed

Combine ingredients. Chill and serve. Garnish with a spear of celery or a kabob of green olives. Makes 6 (6 oz.) servings.

Tomato Tang

2 cans (18 oz. each) tomato juice
¼ cup lemon juice
1 tsp. salt
¾ tsp. Worcestershire sauce
1 drop hot pepper sauce

Combine ingredients and serve. Makes 4 (8 oz.) servings.
ALTERNATIVE: For a lighter, more sippy drink, pour smaller servings and garnish glasses with salt rims.

Snappy Sauer

2½ cups sauerkraut juice
¾ cup tomato juice
1 tsp. lemon juice
1/8 tsp. paprika
½ tsp. horseradish

Combine ingredients and chill. Garnish as desired. Serve very cold. Makes 4 (6½ oz.) servings.

Curried Tomato

¾ cup tomato juice
¾ cup buttermilk
dash curry powder
¼ tsp. salt

Combine ingredients and serve. Garnish with a celery stalk and use as a stir stick. Makes 2 (6 oz.) servings.

Rosy Buttermilk Spice

¾ cup vegetable juice cocktail
¾ cup buttermilk
½ tsp. Worcestershire sauce
1/8 tsp. salt
dash Tabasco

Combine ingredients and serve. Makes 2 (6 oz.) servings.

Cucumber Cuff

1 (12 oz.) can vegetable juice cocktail
¼ cup chopped cucumber
dash garlic powder
6 pimento stuffed olives

Place ingredients in blender to liquefy. Garnish with cucumber slices. Makes 2 (8 oz.) servings.

Clam Shake

6 oz. can clam juice
1/8 tsp. celery salt
1½ tsp. tomato catsup
dashes Tabasco sauce to taste
2-3 ice cubes

Put all ingredients in covered jar and shake vigorously. Strain and serve. Makes 1 serving.

Tomato Twist

1 cup tomato sauce
1 (16 oz.) bottle lemon-lime carbonated beverage

Fill 4 glasses half full of ice. Pour ¼ cup tomato sauce over ice. Fill glass with carbonated beverage. Garnish with twist of lemon. Makes 4 (6 oz.) servings.

Serve this salad with a tomato drink.

Cauliflower Vinaigrette

4 cups thinly sliced cauliflower
1 cup black olives, chopped
⅔ cup green pepper, chopped
½ cup pimento, cut in strips
⅓ cup onions, sliced
½ cup olive oil
3 tbsp. lemon juice
3 tbsp. white wine vinegar
2 tsp. salt
¼ tsp. pepper

Prepare vegetables. Combine dressing ingredients. Pour over vegetables and toss. Cover and refrigerate at least 4 hours before serving. Makes 8 servings.

Clam-Up Cocktail

⅓ cup clam juice
⅓ cup tomato juice
1/8 tsp. celery salt
dashes Tabasco sauce to taste

Put all ingredients in covered jar and shake vigorously. Strain and serve. Makes 1 serving.

Clam Tomato Chill

1 bottle (32 oz.) clam and tomato juice

Chill clamato juice and serve over ice. Garnish with green onion or carrot stick. Makes 4-6 servings.

Clam Kick

2 cups clam and tomato juice
8 oz. soda water
¼ cup lemon juice
Dash hot pepper sauce (optional)

Combine clam and tomato juice and lemon juice. Pour into 4 glasses and add soda water. Stir gently. Makes 4 (6½ oz.) servings.

For hot tomato-based drinks try the following:
Peppy Tomato Cocktail 60
Tomato Juice Warm Up 60
Spicy Tomato Cocktail 61
Vegetable Garni 60
Herbed Vegetable Simmer 61
Mulled Consommé 60

Create with cranberries
Drinks prepared with cranberry juice.

Cranberries have a bitter taste when raw but a pleasantly sharp tang when cooked. The juice is surprisingly refreshing by itself and combines well with most other fruit juices. Its bright color and tart flavor make it a most perfect base for many interesting drinks. To delight your guests, serve cranberry drinks in a chilled or frosted glass and garnish with fresh fruits. Try these recipes and then invent your own using the following guide.

   Really, you can't go wrong with cranberries so experiment! Start with cranberry juice or jellied cranberry sauce.

Add other juices:

apple juice	lemon juice
apple cider	limeade
apricot nectar	lime juice
grapefruit juice	orange juice
grape juice	pineapple juice
lemonade	tea

And/or carbonated beverages:
ginger ale
lemon/lime carbonated
orange carbonated

Or add these spices and heat:

allspice	nutmeg
cardamon	sugar
cinnamon	cinnamon candy
cloves	

For garnishes try:

lemon twist	pineapple
lime twist	orange sherbet
orange slice	lemon or lime sherbet
grapefruit	pineapple sherbet

The following recipes will get you started.

Cranberry Tang

cranberry juice cocktail
lemon

Pour cranberry juice over ice and add fresh lemon to taste. Mix this drink in individual servings.

Cranberry Delight

2   cups cranberry juice cocktail
1½ cups apricot nectar
2   tbsp. lemon juice

Combine chilled juices and serve over ice. Makes 6 (5 oz.) servings.

Cranberry Crash

3   cups cranberry juice
½   cup apricot nectar
2½ tbsp. lemon juice
6   oz. orange carbonated drink

Stir first four ingredients until smooth. Gently add orange carbonated drink. Serve over ice. Garnish with orange slices. Makes 4 (6 oz.) servings.

Cranberry Bracer

cranberry juice
grapefruit juice

Pour equal amounts of each juice over ice and serve. Mix this drink in individual servings.

Cranberry Apple Treat

apple juice
cranberry juice cocktail
lemon

Pour equal amounts apple juice and cranberry juice over ice. Squeeze in lemon juice to taste. Stir. Garnish with pineapple chunks. Make individual servings.

Cranberry Refresher

3   cups cranberry juice cocktail
1   (16 oz.) bottle ginger ale
2   tbsp. lemon juice

Mix cranberry and lemon juices. Just before serving add ginger ale and serve over ice. Garnish with lemon or lime slice. Makes 6 (5½ oz.) servings.

Cranberry Tea Special

2½ cups boiling water
5   tea bags
¾   cup sugar
¼   tsp. cinnamon
¼   tsp. nutmeg
2   cups cranberry juice cocktail
½   cup orange juice
⅓   cup lemon juice

Pour boiling water over tea bags and allow to steep for 5 minutes. Remove tea bags, add sugar to steeped tea and stir to dissolve. Add remaining ingredients and 1½ cups cold water. Cover and cool. Serve well chilled. Makes 6 (5½ oz.) servings.
ALTERNATIVE: For a more predominant cranberry flavor increase cranberry juice to 4 cups and add ¼ tsp. allspice. Makes 10 servings.

Cranberry Fizz I

1 (16 oz.) can chilled cranberry juice
1 (16 oz.) can apple juice
2 tbsp. lemon juice
1 (12 oz.) bottle ginger ale

Combine cranberry juice with apple and lemon juices. Gently add ginger ale. Serve over ice. Makes 8 (6 oz.) servings.

Cranberry Fizz II

For a more predominant cranberry flavor, try this version of fizz.

1 quart cranberry juice cocktail
1 cup apple juice
2 tbsp. lemon juice
1 (28 oz.) bottle ginger ale

Combine fruit juice. Gently add ginger ale. Serve immediately. Garnish with orange slices. Makes 8 (8 oz.) servings.

Sparkling Cider

2 cups cider
1 cup cranberry juice
1 cup sparkling water

Combine ingredients and gently stir. Garnish with a slice of lemon or lime. Makes 4 (8 oz.) servings.

Cranberry Grape Shot

1 quart cranberry juice cocktail
1¼ cup grape juice

Combine ingredients and serve over ice. Makes 6 (6½ oz.) servings.

Pink Velvet

1 cup cranberry juice
⅓ cup orange juice
1 cup vanilla ice cream

Blend and serve. Makes 4 (5 oz.) servings.

Cranberry Crème

2 cups cranberry juice
1 pint orange sherbet
2 tbsp. sugar
1 (12 oz.) bottle ginger ale

Beat cranberry juice and ¾ cup sherbet until smooth. Add sugar and mix. Divide cranberry mixture into 4 servings. Top with ginger ale. Garnish with a dollop of sherbet. Makes 4 (8 oz.) servings.

Cranberry Reviver

1½ cups sugar
2 cups cranberry juice cocktail
1 cup grapefruit juice
2 quarts ginger ale

Combine cranberry juice and sugar, stir until sugar dissolves. Add grapefruit juice. Chill. Gently add ginger ale just before serving. Makes 14 (8 oz.) servings or 28 (punch size) servings.
ALTERNATIVE: Make this with pineapple juice.

Cranberry Snap

½ cup cinnamon candies (red hots)
4 cups boiling water
2 quarts cranberry juice
1 (6 oz.) can frozen limeade concentrate
1 (6 oz.) can frozen orange concentrate

Stir red hots in water until melted. Cool and add cranberry juice and concentrates. Stir to combine. Makes 18 (5 oz.) servings.

Cranberry Orange Sparkle I

1   quart cranberry juice cocktail
1   cup orange juice
2   tbsp. lemon juice
1   (28 oz.) bottle ginger ale

Mix fruit juices. Gently add ginger ale and serve immediately. Garnish with orange or lemon slice. Makes 10 (6½ oz. servings).

Cranberry Orange Sparkle II

1   (16 oz.) can jellied cranberry sauce
¾   cup orange juice
¼   cup lemon juice
1   (28 oz.) bottle ginger ale

Beat cranberry sauce until smooth. Add orange and lemon juice and stir to mix. Gently add ginger ale. Makes 10 (5 oz.) servings.

Hint: To serve a large group, double the recipes for Orange Sparklers. If using a punch bowl, add ginger ale directly to bowl to preserve effervescence.

Cranberry Crush

4   cups cranberry juice
2   cups orange juice
½   cup lemon juice
1   cup pineapple juice
½   cup crushed pineapple
1   cup water
⅓   cup sugar
1   tsp. almond extract

Combine ingredients. Chill and serve over crushed ice. Makes 8 (9 oz.) servings.
ALTERNATIVE: Can also be heated and served warm.

Fruited Punch

1   pint raspberry sherbet
1½ cups sugar
1   cup lemon juice
1½ cup orange juice
1   (32 oz.) bottle cranberry juice cocktail
2   (28 oz.) bottles ginger ale

Mix sherbet, sugar, lemon and orange juice and let stand to soften. Add cranberry juice cocktail. Just before serving, add ginger ale. Serve over ice. Garnish with slices of lemon. Makes 30 (4 oz.) servings.

Cranberry Craze

1   (3 oz.) pkg. cherry flavored gelatin
1   cup boiling water
1   (6 oz.) can frozen lemonade concentrate
2   cups cold water
4   cups cranberry juice cocktail
1   (28 oz.) bottle ginger ale

Dissolve gelatin in boiling water. Add concentrate, cold water and cocktail. Gently add ginger ale and serve. Makes 12 (8 oz.) servings or 24 (4 oz.) punch size servings. For individual servings combine in the following proportions — 2 parts fruit juice mixture: 1 part ginger ale.

Brew a hot one

Hot drinks for appetizers or chilly weather warm-ups.

Break the coffee habit with a hot vege-table or mulled fruit drink. A perfect pick me up! We serve coffee without much thought. Let's keep coffee in our lives but make way for some tastewor-thy alternatives on many occasions. Hot drinks served as appetizers hint of a sumptuous dinner to follow. They are the perfect treat for guests on a chilly evening. There is no better way to wel-come guests than with the aroma of hot cider as they enter your home!

To increase your efficiency as a host/hostess, use all the help you can get from your kitchen equipment. Heat juices in your percolator using the bas-ket to hold spices. No need to strain, simply remove the basket before pour-ing. Hot drinks can be served conveni-ently in 8 oz. mugs with handles.

Mulled Consommé

This can also be served cold over ice.

2 (10¾ oz.) cans beef consommé
1 cup tomato sauce
1 cup water
1/8 tsp. garlic powder

Combine ingredients and heat in sauce pan. Makes 4 generous servings.

Soup Mug

2 (10¾ oz.) cans cream of chicken soup
2 cans water
¼ cup orange juice
pinch of allspice, cloves, nutmeg

Combine ingredients in sauce pan and heat to boiling. Garnish with chopped chives. Makes 4 mug size servings.
ALTERNATIVE: Try this using cream of leek or cream of celery soup.

Peppy Tomato Cocktail

1 (46 oz.) can tomato juice
1 (10¾ oz.) can beef broth
1 tbsp. lemon juice
1 tsp. grated onion
1 tsp. prepared horseradish
1 tsp. Worcestershire sauce
dash hot pepper sauce

Combine and heat ingredients in sauce pan. Garnish with lemon twist or skewered onion. Makes 8 servings.

Aspiring Asparagus

1 (10½ oz.) can cream of asparagus soup
1½ cups milk
½ tsp. celery salt
¼ tsp. ground pepper
3 tbsp. lemon juice

Combine soup and milk and mix until smooth. Add other ingredients. Heat and serve. Garnish with croutons. Makes 4 (5½ oz.) servings.
ALTERNATIVE: May also be served cold, using a celery stalk for garnish.

Beef Brull

2 (10¾ oz.) cans beef broth
1 cup water
2 tsp. horseradish
½ tsp. dill

Combine and heat ingredients in sauce pan. Serve. Makes 4 mug size servings.

Tomato Juice Warm Up

4 cups tomato juice
6 whole cloves
2 tbsp. lemon juice
1½ tsp. sugar
1½ tsp. salt
dash of pepper

Combine and heat ingredients. Makes 4 servings.

Vegetable Garni

4 cups vegetable juice cocktail
¼ cup dairy sour cream

Heat juice in sauce pan. After pouring, add a dollop of sour cream on each serving. Garnish with chopped chives. Makes 4 servings. This is very good served with Rye Krisp.

Herbed Vegetable Simmer

1 **(12 oz.) can vegetable juice cocktail**
1 **(10¾ oz.) can chicken broth**
2 **or more dashes of hot pepper sauce to taste**
¼ **tsp. crumbled basil**

Heat ingredients and let simmer for 5 minutes. Garnish with a pat of butter. Makes 6 servings.

Spicy Tomato Cocktail

1 **(46 oz.) can tomato juice**
1½ **tsp. Worcestershire sauce**
½ **tsp. celery salt**
½ **tsp. salt**
¼ **tsp. oregano or marjoram dash garlic powder**
3 **dashes hot pepper sauce**

Combine and heat ingredients in sauce pan. Garnish with a stalk of celery. Makes 8 servings.

Garlic Toast Crunch

Cut French bread into ½ inch slices. Butter both sides and sprinkle with garlic salt. Toast both sides under broiler. Watch carefully to prevent burning.

Vegetable Dip

½ **cup mayonnaise**
½ **cup dairy sour cream**
1 **tbsp. horseradish**
1 **tbsp. chopped onion**
1 **tsp. Worcestershire sauce**
1 **tsp. chili powder**

Combine above ingredients and refrigerate 4 hours before serving. Serve with raw vegetables such as: carrot and green pepper sticks, celery stalks, cauliflower florets, broccoli buds, red or white radishes, green onions.

Hot Mulled Ciders

After trying these versions of cider you may come up with your original recipe. Brew these concoctions in a percolator and let your guests serve themselves. Set a tray of fresh cookies or warm doughnuts on a side table.

To accompany a cider drink, serve a bowl of sugar lumps which have been tossed with cinnamon.

Garnish your cider drinks with cinnamon sticks, lemon slices, or orange slices.

Cider I

1   **quart cider**
¼   **cup sugar**
2   **(4") cinnamon sticks**
10 **cloves**
8   **whole allspice**
dash of salt

Makes 4 mug size servings.

Cider II

2   **quarts cider**
½   **cup brown sugar**
1   **(4") cinnamon stick**
1   **tsp. whole cloves**
1   **tsp. whole allspice**
1¾ **tsp. nutmeg**
¼   **tsp. salt**

Makes 8 mug size servings.

Cider III

2   **quart cider**
¾   **cup brown sugar**
2   **tsp. cinnamon**
2   **tsp. whole allspice**
1   **tsp. whole cloves**
juice of 2 lemons

Makes 8 mug size servings.

Cider IV

1 **gallon cider**
⅔ **cup sugar**
3 **cinnamon sticks**
2 **tsp. whole allspice**
2 **tsp. whole cloves**

Makes 16 mug size servings.

Cider V

1 **gallon cider**
4 **cinnamon sticks**
10 cloves

Makes 16 mug size servings.

Cider VI

1 **gallon cider**
1⅓ cups brown sugar or honey
4 **cinnamon sticks**
2 **tsp. whole allspice**
1 **tbsp. whole cloves**
2 **tbsp. grated lemon peel**

Makes 16 mug size servings.

ALLSPICE is a small reddish brown berry which has the flavor mixture of cinnamon, clove, nutmeg and juniper.

Cranberry Cider

1 **quart cider**
1 **quart cranberry juice**
½ **cup brown sugar**
6 **cloves**
1 **cinnamon stick**
4 **whole allspice**
dash of salt

Heat, strain and serve. Makes 8 mug size servings.

Jubilee Juice

1 **quart cider**
2 **cups cranberry juice**
1 **cup orange juice**
1½ cups apricot nectar
juice of 1 lemon
1½ tsp. whole cloves

Heat and simmer for 20 minutes. Makes 10 mug size servings.

Snappy Cider

1 **gallon cider**
½ **cup red hot candies**

Heat to dissolve candies. Makes 16 mug size servings.

Mulled Cranberry Swizzle

¾ cup brown sugar
1 cup water
½ tsp. cinnamon
½ tsp. allspice
¾ tsp. ground cloves
¼ tsp. salt
¼ tsp. nutmeg
2 (1 lb.) cans jellied cranberry
    sauce
4 cups unsweetened pineapple
    juice

Combine sugar, salt, spices, and 1 cup water in a saucepan and bring to boil. In separate bowl, beat cranberry sauce, pineapple juice and 3 cups water until smooth. Add to the syrup and simmer 5 minutes. Garnish with butter and cinnamon sticks. Makes 10 servings.

Apricot Delight

1 (46 oz.) can Hawaiian fruit
    punch
1 (46 oz.) can apricot nectar
1 tbsp. lemon juice
6 whole allspice
3 cinnamon sticks

Combine, bring to boil and simmer 10 minutes. Strain and serve. Garnish with clove studded orange slices. Makes 12 servings.

Mulled Pineapple

1 (46 oz.) can unsweetened
    pineapple juice
1 cinnamon stick
1/8 tsp. ground nutmeg
¼ tsp. ground allspice
dash of ground cloves

Combine and bring to boil. Simmer for 30 minutes. Strain and serve. Makes 8 servings.

Hot Spiced Nectar

4 cups apricot nectar
2½ cups orange juice
1 cup water
2 tbsp. lime juice
⅓ cup brown sugar
10 cinnamon sticks
1 tsp. whole cloves

Combine ingredients and simmer uncovered for 15 minutes. Strain and serve. Garnish with fresh slices of lime or lemon. Makes 8 servings.

Honey Apple Tea

1 (16 oz.) can frozen apple juice
    or cider
4 tbsp. instant tea
2 tbsp. honey
1 tsp. cinnamon

Reconstitute cider in sauce pan, add other ingredients. Heat and simmer 5 minutes. Makes 8 servings.
ALTERNATIVE: Substitute 2 quarts apple cider for reconstituted apple juice.

Russian Tea

There are as many versions of this recipe as there are devotees. Basically Russian Tea, or Friendship Tea as it is sometimes called, is a combination of tea, orange and lemonade. The proportions of these three vary according to taste as do the additions of spices and sweeteners.

Make Russian Tea a permanent part of your grocery stock. Mix the dry ingredients and store in an airtight container. For ease in preparation, heat water in an electric percolator. Measure 1½ heaping tsp. mixture into mug, add hot water.

This may be your preferred combination.

2   cups orange powdered breakfast drink
½   cup instant tea powder
1½ cups sugar
1   (3 oz.) pkg. presweetened lemonade mix
1   tsp. cinnamon
½   tsp. ground cloves

Try this version if you prefer less sugar.

2   cups orange powdered breakfast drink
1   cup instant tea powder
1   (3 oz.) pkg. presweetened lemonade mix
1   tsp. cinnamon
1   tsp. ground cloves

Use this recipe if you wish to serve a large group.

½   cup orange powdered breakfast drink
⅓   cup instant tea powder
¼   cup sugar
3   tbsp. presweetened lemonade mix
1   tsp. cinnamon
1/8 tsp. ground cloves

Mix above ingredients and add to 8 cups boiling water. Stir to dissolve. Or brew in electric percolator. Makes 10 servings.

Gift Idea: A decorative glass jar filled with Russian Tea makes a much appreciated gift. Don't forget to label the jar with the recipe.

Insty Orange Drink

2   cups orange flavored instant drink powder
¾   cup instant tea with lemon
1   (3 oz.) pkg. lemon gelatin
1   (3 oz.) pkg. orange gelatin
¾   cup sugar

Mix above ingredients and store in tightly covered container. To serve place 2 heaping tsp. in cup and pour boiling water over. Stir to dissolve.

Hot Chocolate Mix

Try one of these instant chocolate drinks. Mix the following and store in an airtight jar. To serve, simply add hot water.

½ cup instant chocolate mix
2 tbsp. non-dairy creamer
2 tbsp. powdered sugar
½ cup instant milk powder

Place ¼ cup of mixture in 8 oz. serving mug and add hot water. Makes 1 cup of mixture for four servings.

1 (1 lb.) box instant chocolate mix
1 (6 oz.) jar non-dairy creamer
6 tbsp. powdered sugar
8 (1 quart) packets dry milk powder (10¾ cups)

Place ¼ cup of mixture in 8 oz. serving mug and add hot water.

⅓ cup cocoa
2 cups instant milk powder
1 cup sugar
½ tsp. salt

Place ¼ cup of mixture in 8 oz. serving mug and add hot water.

Mocha Mix

1¾ cups instant cocoa mix
¼ cup instant coffee
5½ cups dry milk powder
1 cup non-dairy creamer
1½ tsp. salt

Fill cup or mug half full of mixture and fill with hot water.

Simmering Cranberry

3 cups cranberry juice cocktail
3 cinnamon sticks
6 whole cardamon pods, crushed
¼ tsp. ground allspice
1½ tbsp. butter

Bring cranberry juice and spices to a boil and let simmer for 5 minutes. Strain and add butter. Garnish with clove studded grapefruit slices. Makes 4 (6 oz.) servings. This is particularly good if made a day in advance to allow the flavors to combine. Leave the cardamon in the drink; strain and reheat before serving.

CARDAMON is the fruit of a plant in the ginger family. Powder the plump seeds only as needed for otherwise the aroma loss is great. Use as for cinnamon and cloves.

Chocolate Nog

3 (1 oz.) squares unsweetened chocolate
3 cups milk
1/8 tsp. salt
⅓ cup sugar
½ tsp. cinnamon
1 tsp. vanilla
3 eggs

Combine chocolate and milk in top of double boiler and heat until chocolate melts. Stir. Add salt, sugar, cinnamon and vanilla. Beat the eggs and add to chocolate. Beat until frothy and serve immediately. Makes 4 (8 oz.) servings.

Hot Buttered Exceptionale

Keep this in the freezer for quick individual drinks.

1½ tsp. cinnamon
1 tsp. nutmeg
pinch allspice
1 lb. butter (use the real stuff)
1 lb. brown sugar
1 quart vanilla ice cream

Blend first five ingredients with mixer and add 1 quart softened ice cream. Freeze. To serve put 1 tbsp. mixture in cup and pour hot water over it.

Grapefruit Mull

1   quart grapefruit juice
1½ tbsp. powdered sugar
1   stick cinnamon
1½ tsp. whole cloves

Combine ingredients and heat to simmer. Strain and serve. Makes 4 (8 oz.) servings.

Cranberry Glow

2   cups cranberry juice cocktail
1   lemon, sliced thin
6   cloves
1/8 tsp. nutmeg

Heat to a simmer, taking care not to boil. Garnish with cinnamon sticks. Makes 2 (8 oz.) servings.

Mulled Apricot Nectar

1   (46 oz.) can apricot nectar
½   lemon
3   cinnamon sticks
15 cloves
8   whole allspice

Bring to boil and simmer 5 minutes. Cover and wait 30 minutes before serving. Strain and reheat to serve. Garnish with lemon slices or cinnamon sticks. Makes 8 (6 oz.) servings.

Spicy Grape Drink

1   quart grape juice
6   cups water
¾   cup sugar
1   (6 oz.) can frozen lemonade
     concentrate
1   (6 oz.) can frozen orange juice
     concentrate
3   cinnamon sticks
10 cloves

Heat and simmer for 15 minutes. Strain and serve. Makes 12 (8 oz.) servings or 24 (4 oz.) punch size servings.

Other hot drinks:
Mexi Tomato Garni 52
Honey Lemon Tea 82
Anise Tea 82
Honey Tea 82
Cinnamon Honey Tea 83
Mulled Orange Tea 83
Hot Spiced Tea 84
Mulled Spice Tea 84
Spicy Cider Tea 84
Fruit Brew 83

Embellish your coffee

Fifty alternatives to ordinary black coffee.

Coffee is a universal drink. Its strength and flavor vary from place to place, depending on national custom, the type of coffee beans used and something as seemingly insignificant as the water used in the brewing. Brew coffee to suit your taste or to suit the recipe you are using. For the novice coffee brewer, the procedure for brewing a good pot of coffee is included. The veteran brewer may find some inspirational helpful hints. No matter what the occasion, there is a recipe to help you expand your coffee brewing repertoire from the easy "Cafe Au Lait" to the complex "Coffee Vanilla Delight." Many of these recipes are wonderful dessert drinks. Don't forget the garnishes. Be inventive! Try chocolate shavings, cinnamon sticks, orange or lemon peels. Add your own touch. Make a statement! Anything short of a *rusty nail* will do!

Guidelines for brewing a good cup of coffee

Start with a thoroughly clean coffee-maker. The pot and its parts should be disassembled and cleaned with baking soda. Avoid using a metal scouring pad.

Use the best water available, preferably cold fresh water which has not been chemically treated.

Use a good grade of fresh coffee with a grind suitable to the type of pot to be used — regular, drip or fine.

Brew a full pot of coffee each time.

Avoid boiling coffee while bringing **up to** a boil.

Time your method consistently.

Serve as soon as possible and hold at serving temperature over low heat.

Allow the cream to reach room temperature before serving so it will not cool the coffee.

Store coffee in a tightly closed container away from heat and sun, refrigerating if necessary.

The strength of the coffee is determined by the amount of grounds used in the brewing. The universal coffee formula requires 2 tbsp. of grounds for each cup of water. Brewing for a longer period of time will not strengthen the coffee but only make it bitter. Therefore, if a recipe calls for a strong coffee, use double the amount of grounds in the brewing. If you prefer a weaker coffee use fewer grounds. Once you have determined the coffee strength that suits your taste, be consistent. Use the same pot, the same brewing time and same quantity of grounds each time you brew a pot.

Drip Coffee

2   tbsp. drip grind coffee
1   cup water

Assemble drip pot, placing coffee grounds in coffee section. Pour boiling water into top water section and allow to drip through. When completely dripped, remove top two sections, replace cover and serve.

Percolated Coffee

2   tbsp. drip grind coffee
1   cup water

Place water in pot and bring to boil. Remove from heat and add basket with grounds in it. Cover and return to heat, allowing to percolate gently for 6-8 minutes. Remove basket and serve. Or percolate for 10 minutes with basket of grounds in place. Remove basket before serving.

Steeped Coffee

2   tbsp. regular or fine grind coffee
1   cup water

Pour freshly boiled water over coffee and stir for 30 seconds. Cover and let stand for 5-10 minutes over very low heat. Strain and serve.

Vacuum Method Coffee

2 tbsp. drip grind coffee
1 cup water

Place water in lower bowl of pot. Attach upper bowl securely to pot. Set damp filter in place and add coffee. Heat, bringing water to boil. Stir a few times as water rises to upper bowl, continuing to heat for about 3 minutes. Remove from heat, allowing coffee to return to lower bowl. Remove upper bowl, cover and serve.

Instant Coffee

1 tsp. instant coffee powder
¾ cup water

Add water to coffee. Stir and serve. Or add water to coffee and simmer gently for 2 minutes.

Iced Coffee

coffee
sugar
cream

Prepare coffee and refrigerate in a non-metallic container for not more than 3 hours. Serve over ice, adding sugar and cream to taste.

Quick Iced Coffee

strong coffee
sugar
cream

Brew strong coffee using twice the amount of grounds. Combine equal volumes of ice and coffee and stir to dissolve ice. Serve over ice, adding sugar and cream to taste.

Viennese Coffee

Brew coffee as desired and top with a dollop of whipped cream.

Icy Coffee Cafe

2 cups strong hot coffee
⅓ cup sugar

Combine ingredients and stir until sugar dissolves. Cover and cool and place in freezer. Stir occasionally to prevent mixture from freezing solid. Serve when it reaches consistency of crushed ice. Makes 4 (5 oz.) servings.

Cafe au Lait

strong hot coffee
hot milk
sugar

Simultaneously pour hot beverages from their pots into cups. Add sugar to taste.

Cappuccino Coffee

strong hot coffee
hot milk
cinnamon
nutmeg

Simultaneously pour from two containers into cups. Sprinkle with cinnamon and nutmeg.

Cappuccino Quick

2 cups hot water
1 cup non-dairy creamer
4 cups strong hot coffee
⅓ cup sugar
¼ tsp. nutmeg

Combine water and creamer. Add other ingredients. Garnish with chocolate curls. Makes 8 (8 oz.) servings.

Banana Baron

2 cups strong cold coffee
2 medium sized ripe bananas
⅓ cup evaporated milk
1 (28 oz.) bottle cream soda

Combine coffee, bananas and milk. Beat until smooth and creamy. Pour into serving glasses and fill with very cold soda. Makes 6 (10 oz.) servings.

Creamy Fizzle

2 cups strong cold coffee
½ tsp. bitters
⅓ cup heavy cream
1 (28 oz.) bottle cream soda

Combine coffee, bitters and cream. Pour into serving glasses and gently fill with very cold cream soda. Makes 4 (10 oz.) servings.

Autumn Orange Cafe

4 cups strong hot coffee
2 oranges, sliced thin
¾ cup whipping cream

Pour coffee over oranges and let set for 30 minutes. Strain, reheat and pour into serving mugs. Whip cream, adding sugar if desired. Float a dollop of whipped cream on each cup of coffee. Garnish with orange peel and chocolate shavings. Makes 4 (8 oz.) servings.

White Cap

1 egg white
⅓ cup sugar
⅓ cup whipping cream
4 cups boiling water
2½ tbsp. instant coffee

Beat egg white until frothy. Gradually beat in sugar until stiff meringue forms. In separate bowl whip cream. Fold meringue into whipped cream. Prepare coffee by pouring water over instant powder and stir until dissolved. Put 2 tbsp. meringue into each cup and fill with coffee. Makes 10 (4 oz.) servings.

Honey Brew

½ cup water
1 tbsp. honey
1 tbsp. sesame seeds
3½ tbsp. instant coffee

Heat water, honey and seeds, bringing to a boil. Cover and simmer for 5 minutes. Remove from heat and add coffee. Stir to dissolve. Strain and serve. Makes 2 (4 oz.) servings.

Mocha Nog

1¾ cups boiling water
2 tbsp. dairy creamer
2 tbsp. instant coffee
2 tbsp. sugar
2 eggs
½ tsp. vanilla

Combine dry ingredients, creamer and coffee with water. Stir to dissolve and cool. Beat eggs and vanilla. Fold into coffee mixture. Chill and serve. Makes 2 (10 oz.) servings.

Frost Top Coffee

4 cups strong hot coffee
3 tbsp. honey
2 egg whites

Add honey to coffee and stir. Beat egg whites until soft peaks form adding a little sugar if desired. Beat into hot coffee mixture and serve at once. Makes 5 (6 oz.) servings.

Orange Spice Cafe

2 cups water
1 tbsp. brown sugar
3 cinnamon sticks
thin strip orange peel
¼ tsp. whole allspice
1½ tbsp. instant coffee

Combine all ingredients except coffee and heat to boiling. Strain and pour over coffee. Stir to dissolve coffee. Garnish with slice of orange if desired. Makes 4 (4 oz.) servings.

Creamy Cinnamon

⅔ cup evaporated milk
¼ tsp. vanilla extract
1½ tbsp. confectioners' sugar
½ tsp. cinnamon
2 cups strong hot coffee

Freeze milk in cube tray until crystals form. Chill bowl and beaters. Combine milk crystals, vanilla, sugar and cinnamon in chilled bowl and beat until thick and fluffy. Fill demitasse cups ¼ full of creamy mixture and fill with hot coffee. Garnish with nutmeg. Makes 6 (4 oz.) servings.

Iced Cinnamon Coffee

4 cups strong hot coffee
4 cinnamon sticks
sugar to taste
½ cup heavy cream

Pour coffee over cinnamon and let sit for 1 hour. Remove cinnamon sticks and add sugar to taste. Add cream and chill. Serve over cracked ice. Makes 5 (6 oz.) servings.

Cloved Cafe Frappé

¼ cup very strong coffee
1½ tsp. sugar
dash of ground cloves
2 cups crushed ice
¼ cup water

Blend all ingredients and serve in tall chilled glasses. Makes 2 (10 oz.) servings.

Cardamon Topper

4 cups strong, hot coffee
¼ tsp. ground cardamon
1/8 tsp. mace
¾ cup whipping cream
1 tbsp. sugar
1 tsp. vanilla

Combine coffee, 1/8 tsp. cardamon and mace and keep warm over low heat. Beat whipping cream, sugar and vanilla in chilled bowl until peaks form. Pour coffee into cups and top with whipped mixture. Sprinkle rest of cardamon on topping. Makes 6 (6 oz.) servings or 9 demitasse servings.

Mace is the brightly colored covering of the nutmeg seed. The delicate flavor is unusual and exotic.

Spicy Orange Coffee

1   tbsp. sugar
8   cloves
1   cinnamon stick
peel of 1 orange
1½ cups strong hot coffee

Combine ½ cup water, sugar, cloves, cinnamon stick and peel and simmer for 10 minutes. Strain and add to coffee. Let stand a few minutes before serving. Makes 6 (5 oz.) servings.

Easy Cinnamon Coffee

2   cups boiling water
2   cinnamon sticks
1½ tbsp. instant coffee

Simmer cinnamon sticks in water for 5 minutes. Remove cinnamon and add instant coffee. Stir to dissolve. Garnish with cinnamon stick if desired. Makes 2 (8 oz.) servings.

Mocha International

6   tbsp. instant cocoa mix
¼   cup instant coffee
4   cups boiling water

Pour water over instant powders and stir to dissolve. Garnish with a dollop of sweetened whipped cream. Makes 8 (4 oz.) servings.

Icy Mocha

3   cups cold coffee
3   cups cold cocoa
1½ tsp. vanilla

Combine ingredients and serve over ice. Garnish with sweetened whipped cream. Makes 8 (6 oz.) servings.

Hot Cocoa Coffee

hot coffee
hot cocoa
marshmallows

Combine equal amounts of coffee and cocoa and top with marshmallow.

Mocha Supreme

strong hot coffee
hot chocolate
whipped cream

Pour equal amounts of coffee and chocolate into serving cups and top with whipped cream. Garnish with grated orange peel.

Espresso Leche

1½ tbsp. instant espresso coffee
2 tbsp. instant cocoa mix
2 cups hot milk

Combine ingredients, stirring to dissolve powders. Garnish with cinnamon. Makes 2 (8 oz.) servings.

Mocha Orange

1 cup non-dairy creamer
2 cups hot water
½ cup instant sweet cocoa
2 cups strong hot coffee
2 tsp. grated orange peel

Combine creamer, water and cocoa and cook over low heat until serving temperature is reached. Add coffee and orange peel; simmer for 3 minutes. Garnish with a twist of orange. Makes 6 (6 oz.) servings.

Cinnamon Whip Topping

1 cup whipping cream
2 tbsp. lemon juice
½ tsp. vanilla
¼ tsp. cinnamon
3 tbsp. sugar

Whip cream, gradually adding other ingredients. Continue to whip until soft peaks form. Use in the following recipe:

Marvelous Mocha

2 quarts skim milk
4 squares chocolate
¼ cup instant coffee
¾ cup sugar
¼ tsp. maple extract
1 batch Cinnamon Whip Topping

Combine milk, chocolate, coffee and sugar in sauce pan. Heat and stir until chocolate is melted. Add maple extract. Fold in half of Cinnamon Whip Topping. Pour into mugs and top with remaining topping. Makes 8 (10 oz.) servings.

Midwinter Mocha

1   tbsp. instant coffee
2   tbsp. sugar
2   tbsp. cocoa
pinch of salt
2   cups hot water
2   cups hot milk
1½ tsp. vanilla

Combine coffee, sugar, cocoa and salt and ½ cup hot water. Boil 1 minute. Add milk and remaining water. Reheat to boiling and stir in vanilla. Garnish with marshmallows. Makes 4 (9 oz.) servings.

Cocoa Moco Frost

⅓   cup cocoa
⅓   cup sugar
¼   tsp. salt
½   cup water
4   cup milk
1   pt. coffee ice cream
1½ tsp. vanilla

Combine and heat cocoa, sugar, salt, and water to boiling point. Cook 2 minutes over medium heat, stirring. Add milk and stir until hot. Add vanilla and chill. To serve, pour into glasses and add a scoop of ice cream. Makes 8 (6 oz.) servings.

Southern Mocha

2   tbsp. instant coffee
⅓   cup cocoa powder
2   cups boiling water

Combine ingredients and pour into cups. Garnish with whipped cream, if desired. Makes 4 (5 oz.) servings.

Snow Top Mocha

4   squares chocolate
4   cups hot coffee
⅓   cup sugar
2   tsp. vanilla
2   cups cream

Melt chocolate over hot water. Add hot coffee and sugar and stir until sugar dissolves. Remove from heat and add vanilla. Add 1½ cups whipping cream and beat until very foamy. Pour into serving glasses. Whip remaining cream and place a dollop on each serving. Garnish with a candy cane which can be used as a stir stick. Makes 6 (8 oz.) servings.

Chilled Mocha Froth

2½ cups strong cold coffee
1   pint vanilla ice cream
⅓   cup chocolate syrup
½   tsp. bitters

Combine ingredients and beat until smooth. Serve in iced glasses. Makes 8 (4 oz.) servings.

Coffee Mocha

6   cups strong coffee
⅔   cup chocolate syrup
1½ tsp. vanilla
1   cup whipping cream
4   tsp. sugar
1   pint vanilla ice cream

Combine coffee, syrup and 1 tsp. vanilla and chill. Chill bowl and beaters. In chilled bowl beat cream, remaining vanilla and sugar until soft peaks form. Pour coffee mixture into 6 glasses. Top with a scoop of ice cream and whipped topping. Makes 6 (10 oz.) servings.

Mocha Topping

1 cup whipping cream
½ tsp. vanilla
1½ tbsp. sugar
2 tsp. instant coffee

Whip cream, gradually adding other ingredients until soft peaks form. Makes approximately 1½ cups topping.
Use in the following recipe:

Mocha Mountain Mist

strong hot coffee
coffee ice cream
mocha topping

Pour hot coffee into serving mug and top with a scoop of coffee ice cream and a dollop of mocha topping.

Maxi Mocha

strong cold coffee
milk to taste
chocolate ice cream

Add milk to coffee and stir to mix. Add ice cream and serve. Serve over ice if desired.

Coffee Gate Float

6 cups double strength hot coffee
1 quart vanilla ice cream
1 cup whipping cream

Whip cream, adding sugar as desired. Put 1 scoop ice cream in tall glass. Fill ⅔ full with hot coffee. Add another scoop ice cream and fill with coffee. Top with a dollop of whipped cream and sprinkle with nutmeg. Makes 6 (10 oz.) servings.

Coffee Vanilla Delight

4 cups strong cold coffee
1 cup milk
1 tsp. vanilla
¼ cup sugar
1 quart vanilla ice cream
1 cup whipping cream

Combine coffee, milk, vanilla and sugar and stir until sugar is dissolved. Chill. At serving time place ice cream in glass and pour coffee mixture over it. Whip cream, sweetening with sugar to taste. Place a dollop on each serving. Makes 6 (10 oz.) servings.

Cinnamon Chocolate Mocha

2 cups strong, cold coffee
¼ tsp. cinnamon
½ tsp. vanilla
1½ tbsp. sugar
1 pint chocolate ice cream

Combine coffee, cinnamon, vanilla and sugar and stir to dissolve. Add 1 cup ice cream and mix until smooth. Pour into serving glasses and add remaining ice cream. Garnish with a dollop of whipped cream if desired. Makes 4 (8 oz.) servings.

Mocha Cream

2 tsp. instant coffee
¼ cup boiling water
2 tsp. sugar
pinch of salt
2½ cups milk
1 tsp. vanilla
1 cup chocolate ice cream

Dissolve coffee in water, chill. Stir in sugar, salt, milk and vanilla. Add ice cream and mix until smooth. Makes 4 (8 oz.) servings.

Cafe Pineapple Cream

2½ cups strong cold coffee
2 cups coffee ice cream
1 cup chilled pineapple juice

Combine ingredients and beat until smooth and foamy. Makes 4 (10 oz.) servings.

Butterscotch Mocha Mist

⅓ cup butterscotch topping
¼ cup light cream
2 cups double strength coffee
1 cup coffee ice cream

Combine ingredients and beat until frothy. Makes 4 (6 oz.) servings.

Mocha Banana Float

1 ripe banana
1½ cups strong coffee
½ cup whipping cream
1 tsp. sugar
1½ cups cold milk
1 tsp. vanilla
1 pint coffee ice cream

Mash banana and add coffee, cream and sugar. Beat until well mixed. Add milk and vanilla. Pour into serving glasses and add a scoop of ice cream. Makes 4 (10 oz.) servings.

Dreamy Coffee

1 cup whipping cream
⅓ cup sugar
2 tbsp. instant coffee
1 pint coffee ice cream

Whip cream, gradually adding sugar and coffee. Add ice cream, continuing to beat until blended. Makes 4 (9 oz.) servings.

Festive Mocha Nog

1 cup boiling water
4 tsp. instant coffee
⅓ cup sugar
3 eggs
1 pint chocolate ice cream
2 cups milk
1 cup cream
1 tsp. vanilla

Combine water, coffee and sugar and simmer for 3 minutes. Chill. Separate eggs. Beat egg whites and set aside. Beat yolks until thick and stir into coffee mixture until smooth. Beat in ice cream, add milk, cream, and vanilla. Fold in egg whites. Garnish with shaved chocolate and nutmeg. Makes 6 (10 oz.) servings.

Coffeed Syrup

¼ cup instant coffee
½ cup hot water
2 cups corn syrup
pinch salt
1½ tsp. vanilla

Combine coffee, water, syrup and salt. Simmer for 5 minutes. Skim and add vanilla. Cool and store in covered jar. Refrigerate. Makes 2 cups.
Use in the following recipe:

Coffeed Soda

½ cup Coffee Syrup (see previous recipe)
½ cup heavy cream
1 quart coffee ice cream
club soda

Combine coffee syrup and cream. Pour ¼ cup syrup into tall serving glasses. Add scoops of ice cream. Fill with club soda. Makes 4 (10 oz.) servings.

Other recipes using coffee:

Cafe Tonic 22
Coffee Peach Shake 45
Mocha Mix 66

Start with steeped tea

Iced teas, spiced teas and more.

Tea is an herb brew. A popular mail order catalog offers more than 40 different flavors of tea, ranging from rose hips to wild cherry bark. Believe that? Be exotic and try some of these less conspicuous teas. Then try some variations of the black tea you have been using. Brew any tea by following the simple but important guidelines stated in this chapter. Serve hot or cold. Serve black or add a few mint leaves for a flavor twist or add fruit juices and spices for a Hot Spicy Tea. Perhaps your experiments with tea can start as simply as mine — add a piece of hard candy for sugar and flavor and stir to dissolve. Better yet serve with a dish of candied ginger. Delicious on a chilly day!

Guidelines for brewing that perfect cup of tea

Start with the selection of a clean pot made of glass, china or earthenware.

Use the best water available, preferably fresh cold and naturally soft water which has not been chemically treated.

Heat water in glass or enamel pot.

Warm the teapot by filling it with hot water and emptying it just before adding tea water and leaves.

Bring water just to a full rolling boil before pouring over tea.

Cover the pot and allow tea to steep for 3-5 minutes depending on the strength desired.

Taste to judge the strength of the tea as some weak teas produce a dark brew.

Stir the brew just before serving.

Never steep the leaves more than once.

Store unused tea leaves in a tightly sealed container.

Hot Tea

Follow the previous guidelines for brewing a good cup of tea using the following proportions:

**tea leaves — 1 tsp. leaves for each cup of tea desired plus 1 for the pot
tea bags — 1 bag for each cup desired
instant tea — 1 tsp. for each cup desired**

Hot Tea for a Crowd

**1½ quart cold fresh water
¼ lb. tea leaves**

Bring the cold water to a rolling boil and remove from heat. Add leaves and stir. Allow to steep for 5 minutes and strain into tea pot. To serve pour 1-2 tablespoons of tea syrup into cup and add very hot water from a large pot. Makes 50 servings.

Iced Tea

Brew strong tea, using twice the amount of tea leaves, serve over ice. Add sugar and lemon to taste. Garnish with slice of lemon, lime or sprig of mint.

Sun Tea

**¼ cup tea leaves
3 cups water**

Combine ingredients in glass container, cover and set in sun for a day. Strain and refrigerate overnite. Makes 3 (8 oz.) servings.

Instant Iced Tea

**3-4 tsp. instant powdered tea
3 cups cold water**

Combine ingredients and stir to dissolve. Add sugar and lemon to taste. Garnish as desired. Makes 3 (8 oz.) servings.

Spicy Ice Cubes

3 cups boiling water
5 tea bags
3 cinnamon sticks
10 whole cloves
1 (6 oz.) can frozen lemonade concentrate

Steep spices and tea in boiling water for 5 minutes. Remove tea bags and let sit for 10 more minutes. Strain and add concentrate. Pour into ice cube trays and garnish each section with lemon slice, cherry or a sprig of mint.

Use these cubes in iced tea or fruit drinks.

Minted Iced Tea

bunch of mint
2 cups boiling water
1 quart strong cold tea
sugar to taste

Pour boiling water over mint and steep for 30 minutes. Strain mint brew and add to cold tea. Serve over ice. Garnish with a twist of lemon or a sprig of mint which has been dusted with powdered sugar. Makes 6 (8 oz.) servings.

Tea Caribe

3 cups tea, cooled
1 (6 oz.) can frozen lemonade concentrate
pinch of salt

Combine ingredients and serve over ice. Makes 4 (8 oz.) servings.

Lime Twist

1 quart tea, cooled
juice of 1 lime
¼ cup maraschino cherry juice
1½ tbsp. sugar

Combine ingredients and serve over ice. Garnish with twist of lemon or lime and a cherry. Makes 4 (10 oz.) servings.

Orange Mistea

4 cups tea, cooled
½ (6 oz.) can frozen orange juice concentrate
1 pint orange sherbet

Combine ingredients and mix until well blended. Serve in tall glasses. Garnish with fresh orange slices or cherries. Makes 8 (8 oz.) servings.
ALTERNATIVE: Substitute lemon sherbet for the orange sherbet.

Sparkle Tea Float

⅓ cup instant iced tea powder
2 cups very cold water
1 (12 oz.) can orange carbonated beverage
orange sherbet

Combine tea mix and water and stir until dissolved. Gently add carbonated beverage. Pour into serving glasses and add a scoop of sherbet to each. Makes 4 (8 oz.) servings.
ALTERNATIVES: Can also be made with lemon or raspberry sherbet.

Almond Lemon Tea

3 cups strong tea
1 (6 oz.) can frozen lemonade concentrate
1½ tsp. almond flavoring

Combine ingredients and serve over ice. Makes 4 (8 oz.) servings.

Honey Lemon Tea

1 **quart hot tea**
½ **(6 oz.) can frozen lemonade concentrate**
⅓ **cup honey**
1 **cinnamon stick**

Add ingredients to tea and simmer for 8 minutes. Makes 6 (6 oz.) servings.

Anise Tea

1½ **tsp. anise seeds**
4 **cups cold water**
4 **tsp. tea leaves**

Bring water to boil. Steep tea in 2 cups boiling water for 5 minutes, strain. Meanwhile, steep anise in 2 cups of hot water for 10 minutes, strain. Combine brews and serve while warm. Makes 4 (8 oz.) servings.

Lemon Tea

1 **quart tea, cooled**
½ **(6 oz.) can frozen lemonade concentrate**
½ **cup simple sugar**

Combine ingredients and serve over ice. Garnish with lemon or orange slices. Makes 4 (10 oz.) servings.

Rosy Tea

1 **quart tea, cooled**
2 **cups cranberry juice cocktail**
¼ **cup lemon juice**
1 **tbsp. sugar**

Combine ingredients and serve over ice. Garnish with fresh citrus slices. Makes 6 (8 oz.) servings.

Lemon Tea Mint

2 **quarts strong tea, cooled**
1 **cup mint syrup**
1 **(6 oz.) can frozen lemonade concentrate**

Combine all ingredients and serve over ice. Garnish with slices of orange, lemon or lime or with a sprig of fresh mint. Makes 10 (8 oz.) servings.

Honey Tea

1 **quart hot tea**
⅓ **cup honey**

Combine honey and tea and stir to mix. Serve warm in mugs. Garnish with cinnamon stick and clove studded lemon slice. Makes 4 (8 oz.) servings. For individual servings add 1 tbsp. of honey to each cup of hot tea.

Cinnamon Honey Tea

2 quarts tea
1 (6 oz.) can frozen lemonade concentrate
⅓ cup honey
½ cup sugar
2 cinnamon sticks

Combine all ingredients and simmer for 10 minutes. Serve in mugs. Garnish with slice of lemon or a cinnamon stick. Makes 10 (7 oz.) servings.

Mulled Orange Tea

3 quarts strong tea
1 tbsp. cloves
6 cinnamon sticks
1½ cups orange juice
⅓ cup lemon juice
1 cup honey

Steep tea and spices for 5 minutes, strain. Add juices and honey. Stir to combine. Serve in mugs. Garnish with orange or lemon slices. Makes 14 (8 oz.) servings.

Ginger Mint Tea

2 cups strong hot tea
¼ cup mint leaves
⅓ cup orange juice
¼ cup lemon juice
¼ tsp. powdered ginger
⅓ cup hot water
1 cup cold water

Muddle mint leaves and add tea and juices. In separate container, combine ginger and hot water. Add cold water and mix this with the tea mixture. Chill for 1 hour. Strain and serve. Garnish with fresh mint sprigs. Makes 4 (8 oz.) servings.

Almond Rose Punch

2 quarts strong tea, cooled
1 (6 oz.) can frozen lemonade concentrate
⅓ cup grenadine syrup
1 tsp. almond flavoring

Combine all ingredients. Stir until smooth and serve over ice. Garnish with a kabob of fresh fruit. Makes 8 (10 oz.) servings.

Fruit Brew

1 cup strong tea
1 cup pineapple juice
1 cup orange juice
¾ cup water
1½ tbsp. sugar

Combine all ingredients and heat to boil. Serve in mugs. Garnish with pineapple spears. Makes 4 (8 oz.) servings.

Spicy Cranberry Tea

2½ cups cold fresh water
5 tea bags
½ tsp. cinnamon
¼ tsp. nutmeg
½ cup sugar
2 cups cranberry juice
1½ cups water
½ cup orange juice
⅓ cup lemon juice

Bring 2½ cups cold water to rolling boil and pour over tea, spices and sugar. Steep for 5 minutes. Remove tea bags and stir to dissolve sugar. Let cool. Add other ingredients and chill. Garnish with slices of lemon. Makes 6 (10 oz.) servings.

Hot Spiced Tea

5 cups strong hot tea
½ cup water
¾ cup sugar
¼ cup orange juice
½ cup lemon juice
6 cloves
1 cinnamon stick

Bring water and sugar to a boil, stirring to dissolve sugar. Add other ingredients and simmer for 5 minutes. Strain and serve. Makes 6 (8 oz.) servings.

Mulled Spiced Tea

2 quarts cold fresh water
7 tea bags
½ tsp. whole cloves
1 cinnamon stick
½ cup sugar
½ cup orange juice
¼ cup lemon juice

Bring water to boil and pour over spices and tea. Steep for 5 minutes. Strain. Add sugar and stir to dissolve. Add fruit juices. Serve warm. Makes 8 (8 oz.) servings.

Spicy Cider Tea

2 quarts apple cider
1 quart water
½ cup instant tea
10 whole cloves
2 cinnamon sticks
¼ cup red cinnamon candies
⅓ cup sugar
juice of 1 lemon

Combine all ingredients and simmer for 10 minutes. Stir occasionally to dissolve candies and sugar. Serve in mugs. Makes 12 (8 oz.) servings.

Strawberried Tea

2 quarts strong tea, cooled
1 (6 oz.) can frozen lemonade concentrate
¼ cup sugar
1 (10 oz.) pkg. frozen strawberries

Combine all ingredients and stir until sugar is dissolved and strawberries are broken. Serve over ice. Makes 8 (10 oz.) servings.

Pineappled Tea

¾ cup tea
1 tbsp. lemon juice
1 tsp. sugar
2 tbsp. pineapple juice

Pour all ingredients over ice in tall glass and stir to dissolve sugar. Garnish with lemon twist. Serves 1.

Other recipes using tea are:

Choose a way

To stir and store "insty" drinks from cubes, slushes and powders, to create a cool one from ice cream or sherbet, to keep your calories low. (And a calorie chart, too.)

Stir and store "insty" drinks from cubes, slushes and powders.

Included on this list are those recipes that can be made ahead and stored indefinitely. The cubes can be removed from trays and stored in plastic bags until needed. The slushes, if covered, will keep their fresh taste for several months. The powders can be mixed and stored in air tight jars. These instant powder mixes make very nice and much appreciated gifts. Keep one or more of these "insty drinks" readily available in your kitchen.

Cubes and Slushes
Rosy Slush 38
Frosted Orange Frappé 37
Sweet 'n Tart Cubes 36
Orange Delight 37
Icy Fruit Frappé 49
Après Dinner Fruit Freeze 48
Banana Slushes 48,49
Hot Buttered Exceptionale 67

Powders
Russian Tea 65
Insty Orange Drink 65
Hot Chocolate Mix 66
Mocha Mix 66

Create a cool one from ice cream or sherbet.

This list will enable the ice cream and sherbet connoisseurs to quickly find their delights.

Pineapple Slush 33
Almond Refresher 39
Celebration Frost 33
Strawberry Frost 47
Cranberry Crème 57
Fruited Punch 58
Coffee Gate Float 77
Coffee Vanilla Delight 77
Cinnamon Chocolate Mocha 77
Mocha Cream 77
Festive Mocha Nog 78
Cafe Pineapple Cream 78
Butterscotch Mocha Mist 78
Dreamy Coffee 78
Coffeed Soda 78
Mocha Banana Float 78
Creamy Lemon 21
Berry Shake 30
Chocolate Mountain High 30
Hot Buttered Exceptionale 67
Almond Refresher 39

Peach Pineapple Frappé 45
Coffee Peach Shake 45
Peachy Freeze 45
Pink Velvet 57
Chilled Mocha Froth 76
Coffee Mocha 76
Mocha Mountain Mist 77
Orange Mistea 81
Sparkle Tea Float 81

Keep your calories low.

Clam-Up Cocktail 54
Clam Kick 54
Clam Tomato Chill 54
Day Break Juicer 53
Tomato Toreador 53
Beef Brull 60
Hot Tea 80
Iced Tea 80
Minted Iced Tea 81
Tonic Solo 22
Tonic Refresher 22
Citric Tonic 22
Bitter Lemon Twist 23
Cranberry Bitter 23
Easy Cinnamon Coffee 74
Anise Tea 82

Calorie Chart

Food	Calories
Apple/ 1 small, 2¼" diameter	60
Apple cider/ 1 cup	100
Apple cider/ 1 quart	400
Apple juice/ 1 cup	125
Apple juice/ 1 quart	500
Apricot nectar/ 29 oz. (3½ cups)	490
Avocado/ ½ small	125
Banana/ 1 medium	100
Beef broth/ 10¾ oz. can	80
Bouillon cube/ 1	2
Butter/ 1 tbsp.	100
Carrot, raw, whole/ 1 medium	20
Celery/ 2 stalks	10
Celery soup, cream of/ 10¾ oz. can	185
Cherry juice/46 oz. (5¾ cup)	690
Chicken broth/ 10¾ oz. can	80
Chicken soup, cream of/ 10¾ oz. can	250
Chili pepper/ 1 medium	25
Cinnamon candies/ ½ cup	220
Clamato juice/ 32 oz. (1 quart)	208
Cola/ 16 oz.	210
Consommé/ 10¾ oz. can	80
Cranberry juice cocktail/ 16 oz. can (4 cups)	640
Cranberry sauce, jellied/ 1 cup	530
Cucumber/ 1 medium, 8"	20
Egg, raw, whole/ 1 average	75

Food	Calories
Fruit punch/ 46 oz. (5¾ cup)	690
Gelatin, dessert powder/ 3 oz. pkg.	325
Gelatin, unflavored/ 1 tbsp.	35
Grapefruit, fresh/ ½ medium	75
Grapefruit juice, fresh/ ½ cup	45
Grapefruit juice, canned/ ½ cup sweet	65
Grapefruit juice, canned/ ½ cup, unsweet	45
Grape juice, frozen concentrate/ 6 oz.	300
Grape juice, reconstituted/ 1 cup	100
Honey/ 1 tbsp.	65
Horseradish/ 1 tbsp.	12
Ice cream/ 1 cup	225
Leek soup, cream of/ 10¾ oz. can	250
Lemon/ 1 medium	25
Lemonade/ 1 cup	100
Lemonade, frozen concentrate/ 6 oz.	430
Lemonade reconstituted/ 1 cup	110
Lemonade, powdered mix/ 3 oz. pkg., sweetened	360
Lemon juice/ ½ cup	30
Lemon-lime carbonated drink/ 12 oz.	150
Lime/ 1 medium	20
Limeade, frozen concentrate/ 6 oz.	405
Lime juice/ ½ cup	30
Milk, whole/ 1 cup	165
Milk, powdered/ ½ cup	240
Mushrooms, fresh/ 4 large or 10 small	15

Food	Calories
Nectarines/ 2 medium	60
Olive, green/ 1 medium	7
Olive, ripe/ 1 medium	10
Onion, raw/ 1 medium, 2½" dia.	50
Onion, green scallion/ 5 small	25
Orange, carbonated beverage/ 16 oz.	230
Orange juice, canned/ ½ cup sweet	70
Orange juice, fresh/ ½ cup	50
Orange juice, frozen/ 6 oz.	330
Orange juice, reconstituted/ ½ cup	50
Orange, instant powdered/ 1 cup	800
Parsley/ 1 tbsp.	2
Peach, canned/ 2 halves	75
Peach, fresh/ 1 medium	75
Pear, canned/ 2 halves	85
Pear, fresh/ 1 medium	75
Pear nectar/ 1 cup	130
Persimmon/ 1 medium	100
Pineapple, fresh/ 1 cup	75
Pineapple, canned/ 1 slice, sweetened	75
Pineapple, canned/ 1 slice, unsweetened	78
Pineapple juice, canned/ 1 cup, unsweetened	125
Pepper, green or red/ 1 medium	20

Food	Calories
Prune juice/ ½ cup	85
Radish/ 1" dia.	2
Raspberries, canned/ ½ cup	100
Raspberries, fresh/ ½ cup	35
Raspberries, frozen, sugar added/½ cup	120
Rhubarb, fresh/ 4 cups unsweetened	80
Rhubarb, stewed/ ½ cup sweetened	175
Sherbet/ 1 cup	235
Soda water/	0
Sour cream/ ¼ cup	120
Strawberries, fresh/ 10 large	40
Strawberries, frozen, sugar added/ ½ cup	117
Sugar, brown/ 1 tbsp.	50
Sugar, powdered/ 1 tbsp.	40
Sugar, white/ 1 tbsp.	50
Sugar, white/ ½ cup	480
Tangerine/ 1 large or 2 small	45
Tomato, fresh/ 1 medium	25
Tomato juice/ 1 cup	50
Tomato sauce/ ½ cup	160
Tonic water/ 10 oz. bottle	5
Vegetable juice cocktail/ ½ cup	20
Yogurt/ 1 cup	130

Mixology charts

We'll assume you've read through this volume of joyous juices. You are inspired to mix an unusual brew, but a search of your cupboards and refrigerator yields only orange juice, cider and lemon. A thirsty pack of friends is about to lunge through your living room. What can you do? Use these charts which will help you create a stunning beverage without dashing to the grocery store. Locate the ingredients you hold in your hand on the list at the right, read across to the black dots, follow the column down to the recipe title (or titles) which use those ingredients. And — presto — happy, contented guests and an intact reputation as an imaginative host/hostess.

ginger ale
club soda
tonic water
cola
root beer
bitter lemon
grape juice
orange juice
cider
cranberry juice
pineapple juice
lemon juice
lime juice
coffee
tea

Root Beer Twist
Cola Coda
Cola Swirl
Black and White
Pineapple Frost
Frosted Herb Nectar
Cranberry Bitter
See also Chapter I
Iced Tea Tonic
Café Tonic
Citric Tonic
See also Chapter I
Lemon Fizz
Grape Fizz
See also Chapter I
Bitter Breeze
Pineapple Orange Fizzle
Cranberry Orange Fizzle
Grape Fizzle
Orange Cooler
Grape Zest
See also Chapter I

Row labels (right side):
- egg
- grape juice
- frozen grape conc.
- orange juice
- frozen orange conc.
- cider
- pineapple juice
- lemon juice
- lime juice
- frozen lime conc.
- grape fruit juice
- milk
- yogurt
- buttermilk

Column labels (bottom):
- Pineapple Passion
- Strawberry Passion
- Buttermilk Nectar
- Yogurt Puff
- Orange Yogurt
- Strawberried Yogurt
- Chocolate Mountain High
- Iced Chocolate Milk
- Chocolate Milk
- Orange Milk
- Berry Shake
- Rose Petal
- Prairie Popper
- Orange Nog
- Cider Nog
- Egg Nog
- Orange Derby
- Golden Lemon Break
- Pink Lemorange
- Herbed Pineapple Froth
- Lime Beauty
- Bitter Lime
- Sweet Charity
- Crackling Grape
- Sunrise Cocktail
- Rosy Lady
- Apricot Pleasure
- Orange Twist
- Rising Moon
- Purple Stem
- Hawaiian Haste
- Pineapple Rouge
- Pineapple Snow
- Crackling Fruitail
- Lime Slush
- Tropical Orange Crush
- Gulf Crush
- Lemon Daisy
- Lemon Sour
- Lemonade

91

	orange juice	apricot nectar	pineapple juice	grapefruit juice	cherry juice	fruit punch	apple juice	pineapple concentrate	orange juice concentrate	lemon concentrate	grape juice	lemon juice	lime juice	ginger ale	lemon/lime carbonate	soda water
Lemonade Rose										•						
Pineapple Chunk	•		•									•	•	•		•
Black Cherry Charge										•						•
Fruit Frolic						•										•
Fruited Julep				•							•			•		
Almond Refresher													•		•	
Lemon Horizon												•	•			•
Orange Delight	•													•	•	
Raspberry Orange Fizz	•														•	
Sweet 'n Tart Cubes			•												•	
Frosted Orange Frappé	•											•		•		
Rosy Slush	•											•		•		
Mint Lemonale												•		•		
Lemon Sparkle								•		•				•		
Fabulous Fizz										•				•		
Twisted Apricot Nectar		•								•				•		
Sparkling Nectar	•	•										•		•		
Fruit Sparkle	•		•									•		•		
Gingermint			•									•		•		
Grande Grape	•										•			•		
Orange Lemonale	•											•		•		
Sparkling Fruit Drink	•			•										•		
Orange Jubilee									•					•		
Orange Pineapple Pleasure							•	•						•		
Lime Lighter			•											•		
Celebration Frost		•						•	•	•		•		•		
Pineapple Slush			•											•		
Pineapple Cherry Bubble			•		•							•		•		
Rosied Ale						•						•		•		
Tropical Treat			•							•				•	•	
Great Grape	•		•								•	•		•		
Ginger Ale Gala			•						•			•		•		

	Pineapple Pleasure	Congeniality Party Punch	Reformation Tea	Fruited Tea Punch	Ciderbelle	Betsey Cider	Super Orange	Lemonade Royale	July Julep	Grape Gala	Summer Jubilee	Fruit Supreme	Pineapple Surprise	Apricot Orange Drink	Frosty Lady
orange juice					●	●			●			●		●	●
apricot nectar													●	●	
pineapple juice					●								●	●	
apple juice										●	●	●			
cider					●									●	
pineapple concentrate				●											
orange juice concentrate			●				●								
lemon concentrate		●	●								●	●			
lime concentrate			●												
grape juice								●	●	●					
lemon juice		●			●				●					●	
lime juice										●					●
ginger ale		●	●	●											
lemon/lime carbonate	●														

coffee
orange juice
apricot nectar
pineapple juice
fruit punch
milk
orange juice concentrate
lemon concentrate
lemon juice
lime juice
ginger ale
lemon/lime concentrate

Hot Spiced Nectar
Mulled Pineapple
Apricot Delight
Peach Pineapple Frappé
Raspberry Rag
Pineapple Carrot Tip
Strawberry Melon Jubilee
Raspberry Celebration
Banana Frappé
Banana Slush II
Banana Slush I
Fresh Fruit Shake
Apres Dinner Fruit Fresh
Icy Fruit Frappé
Strawberries Afloat
Orange Strawberry Ale
Strawberry Frost
Strawberry Cobbler
Coffee Peach Shake
Icy Peach Blend
Peach Starter
Peachy Freeze
Rhubarb Sparkler
Rhubarb Refresher
Raspberry Mint Twist

	Herbed Vegetable Simmer	Vegetable Garni	Spicy Tomato Cocktail	Tomato Juice Warm Up	Peppy Tomato Cocktail	Mulled Consommé	Clam-up Cocktail	Clam Shake	Cucumber Cuff	Clamato Kick	Clam and Tomato	Tomato Twist	Rosy Buttermilk Spice	Curried Tomato	Day Break Juicer	Snappy Sauer	Celeried Tomato	Tomato Tang	Tomato Toreador	Herbed Consommé	Basiled Beef	Sparkling Tomato Cocktail	Tomato Pow	Mexi Tomato Cocktail	Tomato Juice Cocktail
tomato juice		•	•	•		•								•	•	•	•	•	•	•	•	•	•	•	•
lemon juice										•								•				•			
lime juice																						•			
sauerkraut juice																•									
grapefruit juice															•										
veg-juice cocktail	•	•							•				•												
tomato sauce						•						•													
clam and tomato juice										•	•														
clam juice							•	•																	
buttermilk													•	•											
beef consommé or consommé					•	•														•	•				
lemon/lime carbonate												•										•			
soda water										•															

cranberry juice

grapefruit juice

lemon juice

apple juice

apricot nectar

orange juice

lime conc.

orange concentrate

pineapple juice

grape juice

lemonade concentrate

cider

ginger ale

Banana Cream
Grapefruit Mull
Spicy Grape Drink
Mulled Apricot Nectar
Cranberry Glow
Simmering Cranberry
Jubilee Juice
Cranberry Cider
Snappy Cider
Hot Mulled Cider
Cranberry Craze
Fruited Punch
Cranberry Cream
Pink Velvet
Cranberry Grape Shot
Cranberry Orange Sparkle II
Cranberry Orange Sparkle I
Cranberry Crush
Cranberry Snap
Cranberry Reviver
Sparkling Cider
Cranberry Fizz II
Cranberry Fizz I
Cranberry Crash
Cranberry Delight
Cranberry Refresher
Cranberry Apple Treat
Cranberry Bracer
Cranberry Tang

Ingredient columns (top chart): coffee, instant coffee, non-dairy creamer, whipping cream, cream, chocolate squares, milk

Recipes (top chart): Festive Mocha Nog, Cafe Pineapple Cream, Butterscotch Mocha Mist, Coffeed Syrup, Coffeed Soda, Mocha Banana Float, Chocolate Nog

Ingredient columns (bottom chart): coffee, instant coffee, non-dairy creamer, whipping cream, cream, chocolate squares, milk

Recipes (bottom chart): Iced Coffee, Viennese Coffee, Icy Coffee, Cafe Au Lait, Cappuccino Coffee, Cappuccino Quick, Banana Baron, Creamy Fizzle, Autumn Orange Cafe, White Cap, Honey Brew, Mocha Nog, Frost Top Coffee, Orange Spice Cafe, Cloved Cafe Frappé, Iced Cinnamon Coffee, Creamy Cinnamon, Spicy Orange Coffee, Easy Cinnamon Coffee, Cardamon Topper, Mocha International, Icy Mocha, Hot Cocoa Coffee, Mocha Supreme, Espresso Leche, Midwinter Mocha, Marvelous Mocha, Mocha Orange, Snow Top Mocha, Southern Mocha, Cocoa Moco Frost, Chilled Mocha Froth, Coffee Mocha, Coffee Gate Float, Mocha Mountain Mist, Marvelous Mocha, Coffee Vanilla Delight, Cinnamon Chocolate Mocha, Mocha Cream

	coffee	tea	orange concentrate	lemon concentrate	lime concentrate	pineapple concentrate	grape concentrate	honey	pineapple juice	orange juice	cranberry juice	lemon juice	cherry juice	lime juice	cider	ginger ale
Cinnamon Honey Tea		•		•				•								
Honey Tea		•						•								
Lemon Tea Mint		•		•												
Rosy Tea		•									•	•				
Almond Lemon Tea		•			•											
Sparkle Tea Float	•	•														
Orange Mistea		•	•													
Lime Twist		•											•	•		
Tea Caribe		•			•											
Lemon Tea		•			•											
Anise Tea		•														
Honey Lemon Tea		•		•				•								
Minted Iced Tea		•														
Rhubarb Royale		•														
Insty Orange Drink		•														
Russian Tea		•														
Honey Apple Tea		•						•							•	
Congeniality Party Punch		•		•			•					•				•
Reformation Tea		•	•	•			•									•
Fruited Tea Punch		•		•	•	•					•					•
Cranberry Tea Special		•								•	•	•				
Pineappled Tea		•							•			•				
Strawberried Tea		•			•											
Fruit Brew		•							•	•						
Spicy Cider Tea		•										•			•	
Mulled Spiced Tea		•								•		•				
Hot Spiced Tea		•								•		•				
Spicy Cranberry Tea		•								•	•	•				
Almond Rose Punch		•		•												
Ginger Mint Tea		•								•		•				
Mulled Orange Tea		•						•		•		•				

Index